D1120619

THE BLUE RIBBON COOK BOOK

THE
BLUE RIBBON
COOK BOOK

JENNIE C. BENEDICT

Introduction by Susan Reigler

UNIVERSITY PRESS OF KENTUCKY

Paperback edition 2022
Copyright © 2008 by The University Press of Kentucky

Scholarly publisher for the Commonwealth,
serving Bellarmine University, Berea College, Centre
College of Kentucky, Eastern Kentucky University,
The Filson Historical Society, Georgetown College,
Kentucky Historical Society, Kentucky State University,
Morehead State University, Murray State University,
Northern Kentucky University, Spalding University,
Transylvania University, University of Kentucky, University
of Louisville, and Western Kentucky University.
All rights reserved.

Editorial and Sales Offices: The University Press of Kentucky
663 South Limestone Street, Lexington, Kentucky 40508-4008
www.kentuckypress.com

Library of Congress Cataloging-in-Publication Data

Benedict, Jennie C. (Jennie Carter), 1860–1928.
 The blue ribbon cook book / Jennie C. Benedict ; introduction by
Susan Reigler.
  p. cm.
 Reprint. Originally published: Louisville, Ky. : The Standard Printing
Co., 1922.
 Includes index.
 ISBN 978-0-8131-2518-3 (hardcover : alk. paper)
 1. Cookery, American. 2. Menus. I. Title. II. Title: Blue ribbon
cookbook.
 TX715.B47 2008
 641.5973—dc22
                    2008026766
 ISBN 978-0-8131-9533-9 (pbk. : alk. paper)

This book is printed on acid-free paper meeting
the requirements of the American National Standard
for Permanence in Paper for Printed Library Materials.

Manufactured in the United States of America.

 Member of the Association of
University Presses

INTRODUCTION

Susan Reigler

The dedication to the fifth edition of *The Blue Ribbon Cook Book*, published in 1938, reads: "We who knew and loved her were proud of her business success; proud that she ranked with the highest in her profession, and consulted and was consulted by Oscar of New York, Jacques of Chicago, Harvey of Washington, and others almost as famous. Of all these things we were proud for her sake, but our greatest pride lay in just knowing the splendid courageous and noble little woman whom we called 'Miss Jennie.'"

"Miss Jennie" was Jennie C. Benedict, born in Harrods Creek, Kentucky, near Louisville, in 1860. By the turn of the century, she had become Louisville's foremost caterer. With the combination of her culinary education (she studied with Fannie Farmer at the Boston Cooking School for six weeks in the 1890s) and a thorough knowledge of local traditions, Miss Jennie shaped the tastes of the city. She catered the parties and weddings of Louisville's most prominent citizens. Customers from the growing middle class patronized her downtown tearoom, which expanded to its second and final location in the 500 block of South Fourth Street in 1911.

Benedict began her career in 1893 from her family's home at Third and Ormsby streets. In her autobiography,

Road to Dream Acre, published in 1928, she recounted paying a builder the "stupendous" fee of $316.85 to add a 256-square-foot kitchen with a 48-square-foot pantry onto the house. (It did not, by the way, have running water.) Her "start in business," as she recalled, was effected by fruitcake.

She was soon meeting customers' demands for far more than fruitcake, however. Miss Jennie supplied the first school lunches in the city—chicken salad sandwiches sold to students from a pushcart. Menus featuring both her sweet and savory dishes became the centerpieces of parties, not least of which, since she was plying her trade in Louisville, were those thrown on Derby Day. The depth of her recipe repertoire was documented with the publication of the first edition of *The Blue Ribbon Cook Book* in 1904. Now, more than a century later, Jennie Benedict's popular recipes are once again available, with this reprint of the fourth edition, which dates from 1922.

With literally thousands of cookbooks on bookstore shelves, why reprint this one? Quite simply, there is a call for it. Over the decades, copies of *The Blue Ribbon Cook Book* have "disappeared" from regional libraries. A generous cook often found that the copy loaned to a neighbor was never returned. During my fourteen years as restaurant critic at the *Louisville Courier-Journal* (the newspaper at which, decades earlier, Miss Jennie enjoyed a brief stint as editor of "household items"), I had many, many calls from readers trying to locate a copy of the cookbook, as did my colleague, former food editor Sarah Fritschner. This continuing interest may come from the fact that so many familiar Louisville flavors seem to have their origins (or reach their definitive versions) in Jennie Benedict's recipes.

I was born in the middle of the twentieth century, but I vividly remember as a young adult encountering such party foods as tomato jelly and supreme of chicken, found in this cookbook on pages 90 and 75, respectively. Cheese and nut sandwiches very much like the ones described on page 97 were a staple for decades at the restaurant in the now-closed Stewart's Dry Goods on Fourth Street in downtown Louisville. (Yes, I also remember, as a little girl, having to wear white gloves when we went downtown to shop! That surely was an echo of Miss Jennie's time, a social custom that endured for decades.) A very close iteration of the stuffed eggplant on page 72 has been a fixture of the menu at Simpsonville's Old Stone Inn for as long as I can remember. Another taste of culinary history, Benedict's popular chicken salad of school lunch sandwich fame, is on page 96. Benedict's mayonnaise was extremely popular and sold by the jar in her store. A key ingredient in many of her sandwich and salad dressing recipes, you'll learn how to make it on page 93. The fruitcake recipe that started it all is on page 112.

The Blue Ribbon Cook Book isn't just a repository of food history; it's a very practical cookbook, easy to use, with lots of shortcuts, kitchen tricks, and tips on cooking technique from Miss Jennie. Most of these are in the glossary at the front of the book. One of my favorites is: "To REMOVE the odor of onions from the hands, crush parsley in the fingers." Not surprisingly, some ingredients in Benedict's recipes, such as lard, are no longer widely used, and many, including ammonia powder, sound downright mysterious. Depending, of course, on how authentic you want to be, lard is still obtainable at many butchers' counters. Ammonia powder (once a widely used leavening agent) is ammonium bicarbonate.

You can get it from a pharmacy, but you'll need to grind it into a powder. Simply use baking soda instead. For any dish that requires "zephyrette" crackers, go ahead and substitute saltines.

Happily, making coffee is far easier today than in the first half of the twentieth century. Miss Jennie's instructions on page 133 involve the use of a beaten egg and its broken shell for clarifying the brew. The addition of cold water to the hot coffee is suggested to capture grounds and make them sink. (There's an entire lesson in physical chemistry within this one-paragraph recipe.)

No small part of the charm of *The Blue Ribbon Cook Book* is Miss Jennie's voice, which is very clear and, in places, uncannily similar to that of a later American cookbook author, Julia Child. One example, Miss Jennie's no-nonsense advice on serving wine, still makes me grin. It was included in the fifth edition, but not the fourth, since the 1922 book was published during Prohibition. "In the first place, let us state boldly that much of the discouragingly elaborate instructions we hear about wine is pretty shrewd propaganda on the part of foreign growers. Without questioning the quality of their products we can still know that we make splendid wines in this country—wines good enough for anyone, however 'expert' they may be." Were she alive today, Miss Jennie might be pleasantly surprised to find more than seventy vineyards and wineries located in her home state.

In addition to her strong opinions, Miss Jennie was known for helping ordinary cooks prepare for elaborate functions. In this book, you'll find menus under the headings "Formal Dinner," "Informal Dinner" and "Simple Luncheon," all of which list far more dishes and courses than are served in most homes today. But you can pick and choose. Just refer to the alphabetical index for individual recipes. Many would be perfect to include in a "Miss Jennie's Derby Brunch" menu that you create based on her dishes.

A true historical curiosity of *The Blue Ribbon Cook Book* is an entire chapter entitled "Sick Room Cookery." (You will not see that in a modern cooking tome!) Providing recipes meant to hasten recovery from illness, this one may not prove as enduring as other chapters. It's hard to imagine any twenty-first century patient being cheered by the raw meat diet (page 148) or rallying upon being served a tray containing creamed calf brains (page 153). Don't read the recipe for peptonized oysters (page 150) if you are already feeling a bit queasy. On the other hand, the cocoa cordial listed on the same page, made with chocolate and port ("useful in cases of chill or exhaustion"), might just hit the spot. It is interesting that certain alcoholic ingredients used for medicinal purposes seem to have slipped into this Prohibition edition of the cookbook.

The cookbook's other chapters contain more than 300 recipes for breads, soups, fish, meats, vegetables, entrees, sandwiches, sauces, salads, salad dressings, and desserts. Found in the "Miscellaneous" chapter are such savories as anchovy eggs and green tomato pickles. Ironically, the recipe for which Jennie Benedict is almost exclusively remembered today is not found in any of the five editions of her cookbook, nor among the recipes included in her autobiography. Benedictine spread, the famous eponymous sandwich ingredient made with cucumber juice and cream cheese, is still very much a part of Louisville's culinary scene. Cookbook author Ronni Lundy, in her *Shuck Beans, Stack Cakes, and Honest Fried Chicken* (Atlantic Monthly Press, 1991), perfectly describes the circumstances in which generations of Louisvillians have encountered Benedictine:

> Classically Benedictine Cheese is spread thinly between pieces of soft white bread with the crusts trimmed, then cut in diagonal fourths and served on a doily-covered platter. That recipe uses just the juice from the cucumbers and onions to make a smooth spread.
>
> Recently, though, local cooks have started to add the drained, grated cucumber back into the mix. One Louisville restaurant also makes a fat, earthy Benedictine with small chunks of unpeeled cucumber and pieces of red onion through the flavored and colored cheese. The chunkier spreads go well with hearty, whole wheat bread.

The recipe Lundy gives is surely the one Miss Jennie would have published in *The Blue Ribbon Cook Book* if she had decided to include it (and we really have no idea why she didn't). It's certainly the version I recall from decades ago:

> 8 ounces of cream cheese, softened
> 3 tablespoons cucumber juice
> 1 tablespoon onion juice
> 1 teaspoon salt
> a few grains of cayenne pepper
> 2 drops green food coloring
>
> To get the juice, peel and grate a cucumber, then wrap in a clean dish towel and squeeze juice into a dish. Discard pulp. Do the same for the onion. Mix all ingredi-

ents with a fork until well blended. Using a blender will make the spread too runny.

As Lundy mentions, some Louisville restaurants have embraced Benedictine, which seems perfectly appropriate given Miss Jennie's pioneering place in the city's early restaurant and entertaining landscape. Kathy Cary, who is in many ways a modern-day Jennie Benedict, being both a restaurateur and a much-in-demand caterer, told me that she owns a well-loved, very battered and stained copy of *The Blue Ribbon Cook Book*. Her restaurant, Lilly's, located on Bardstown Road (Louisville's entertainment hub today much as Fourth Street was in Jennie Benedict's day), serves a signature sandwich of Benedictine and bacon at lunchtime. Here are Cary's recipes for both the spread and the sandwich, which she graciously provided for use here:

LILLY'S BENEDICTINE

8 ounces cream cheese
1 cucumber, peeled, seeded, finely chopped
2 tablespoons red onion, finely chopped
¼ teaspoon kosher salt
¼ teaspoon freshly ground black pepper
1 tablespoon fresh dill, finely chopped

Bring cream cheese to room temperature. Add other ingredients and mix well.

LILLY'S BENEDICTINE AND BACON SANDWICH

Spread homemade mayonnaise (flavored with mustard, salt, cayenne) on two slices of quality whole wheat bread.

Layer with Benedictine, and top with applewood-smoked bacon; close sandwich, and serve.

Another excellent example of the creative use of Benedictine is found a bit further along Bardstown Road at the Uptown Café, where it provides a distinctly Louisville variation on the tradition of serving salmon with cream cheese. Many thanks go to proprietor Kelley Ledford and chef Matt Weber for the Uptown's recipes, which will yield enough canapés for a large dinner party:

UPTOWN CAFÉ'S BENEDICTINE

6 cucumbers, peeled and seeded. Puree in food
    processor and drain well.
3 pounds softened cream cheese
½ yellow onion, diced
1 lemon, juiced
1 teaspoon salt
2 teaspoons white pepper
5 shots Tabasco

Process onion; add softened cream cheese and process until smooth. Add everything else and process again.

UPTOWN CAFÉ'S SMOKED SALMON CANAPÉS

Spread a thin layer of Benedictine on pieces of toasted marble rye cut diagonally into quarters. Add a sprinkling of diced red onion and small pieces of smoked salmon. Top each canapé with a slice of cucumber and sprinkle with capers.

While Benedictine is almost exclusively found in the Louisville area, some Derby City expatriates have helped introduce the spread to other locales. The Holly Hill Inn in Midway, Kentucky, features Benedictine thanks to sous-chef and former Louisvillian Lisa Laufer, who fondly recalls taking Benedictine sandwiches to school for her lunch. Holly Hill's chef/owner Ouita Michel used Laufer's Benedictine recipe when she cooked at the James Beard House in New York City. There, Benedictine was served on silver-dollar-size corn cakes with Shuckman's smoked trout, chives, and lemon zest. Laufer's recipe also works well with other smoked or cured fish and hickory-smoked bacon. Laufer supplied the recipe for her variation of Benedictine for this book, and she offers a great tip for using leftover cucumber juice.

THE LAUFER FAMILY BENEDICTINE
(used at Holly Hill Inn)

1½ pounds cream cheese
4 large cucumbers (or 6 if they seem small)
onion juice to taste (start with 1 teaspoon)
1 teaspoon salt or more to taste
3 to 4 dashes of Crystal Hot Sauce

Soften the cream cheese to room temperature. Peel the cucumbers, leaving a little bit of skin on for color. Puree them in a food processor. Squeeze the cucumber pulp in cheesecloth until it is as dry as possible. Discard the juice (or use it in a cocktail; cucumber juice is delicious in a Bloody Mary or chilled with a splash of lemon and vodka). For the onion juice, grate ¼ of a peeled onion and squeeze in cloth to remove the juice. Combine cucumber and onion pulp with remaining ingredients. Check the seasonings. Note: No food coloring or mayonnaise is used in this recipe.

Louisville's current residents don't have to spend time in the kitchen whipping up any of the variations of Benedictine printed here. Virtually every independently owned grocery store and gourmet-to-go food shop/deli sells made-on-the-premises Benedictine by the cup, the pint, and the quart. Such is the local demand for Benedictine that you will also find it at many Louisville locations of national supermarket chains. Notable Benedictines are made at Burger's Supermarket in the Highlands, the Cheddar Box Café in St. Matthews and Middletown, and Mike Best's Meats and Deli in the Brownsboro Road area. All three establishments make Benedictine sandwiches for their customers.

Miss Jennie's Benedictine, fruitcake, and other delicacies propelled her to become one of Louisville's leading businesswomen. She was also known for her work on behalf of charities, especially as a founder of the King's Daughters, a group of women who volunteered to nurse Louisville's sick among the poor. In 1925, after more than thirty years cooking professionally, Miss Jennie sold her business for about $50,000 and retired to a house on a bluff overlooking the Ohio River just east of Louisville. She named it Dream Acre. At a King's Daughters convention in 1928 she became ill and soon after died of pneumonia at the age of sixty-eight. She is buried in Louisville's Cave Hill Cemetery.

Miss Jennie's connection to Louisville endures as a testament to her love for the city, and the love of the city's residents for her. At the height of her career, some citizens of St. Louis reportedly offered Miss Jennie $1 million to move her operations to their city. There was an uproar when word of this was circulated in Louisville. City officials, church leaders, and her loyal customers all begged Miss Jennie to stay. Apparently, this outpouring of community love triumphed over money. She remained in Louisville.

Louisville native SUSAN REIGLER was the restaurant critic for the *Courier-Journal* from 1992 to 2006. She lives in Louisville, where she has ready access to a seemingly endless supply of Benedictine.

THE BLUE RIBBON COOK BOOK

BEING

A FOURTH PUBLICATION OF "ONE HUNDRED
TESTED RECEIPTS," TOGETHER WITH
MANY OTHERS WHICH HAVE BEEN
TRIED AND FOUND VALUABLE

BY

JENNIE C. BENEDICT

"'Tis an ill cook that cannot lick his own fingers."
—SHAKESPEARE: *Romeo and Juliet.*

THE STANDARD PRINTING CO.
LOUISVILLE

COPYRIGHT
JENNIE C. BENEDICT
1922

PREFACE

In offering to the public the fourth edition of my Cook Book, I do so earnestly hoping and believing that the contents will help to solve problems in many homes.

After thirty years of study, teaching and catering, I have tried to embody in this edition, the very best of all that I have in recipes, including a number from the late Miss Fannie Merrit Farmer, Principal of the Boston Cooking School, under whom I studied. I have tried to give the young housekeeper just what she needs, and for more experienced ones, the best that can be had in the culinary art.

I have included a number of recipes for dishes for the sick and convalescents, with a few choice menus for luncheons and dinners.

JENNIE C. BENEDICT

INDEX

BREAD

SOUP GARNISHINGS

FISH

MEATS

CAKES

FILLINGS FOR CAKES

ICES

MISCELLANEOUS

SICK ROOM COOKERY

MENUS

GLOSSARY

MARINATE.—To make salads successfully, the meat or celery or nuts should be placed in a dish and covered with three parts oil and one part vinegar, and a little salt, which is to marinate for several hours. Then any of the dressing which is n o t absorbed should be drained off, the salad mixed as desired, and the regular dressing poured over it.

BROWN STOCK.—To make brown stock successfully, take a four-pound soup bone, remove some of the meat from the bone, and then place the bone in the soup kettle with three quarts of cold water and let it boil on the back of the stove. Take the soup vegetables with a little parsley and two cloves and the meat which you have reserved from the soup bone, chop all fine and saute until brown. Pour into the boiling kettle and let all boil together slowly five or six hours. Remove from the fire, strain through a fine sieve, let it cool, and skim off the grease. Put away in a cool place and use as desired.

WHITE STOCK.—Take the liquor in which chicken or veal has been boiled, remove the meat and season, boil for fifteen minutes with a stalk of celery, a slice of onion, two slices of carrot and a bay leaf, and a little salt and pepper. Strain and use as white stock.

CAKE.—To obtain t h e best results in making cake where milk and baking powder are to be used, stir into the milk the baking powder and add to the cake the last thing, for in many cases, where the baking powder is put into the flour, some of it is lost—and the cake is not as light as it should be.

CAKE.—In plum puddings, fruit cakes, mince meats, etc., where spices and liquor are used, I find it more desirable to let the spices stand in the liquor for an hour or more before putting into the other ingredients.

WHIPPED CREAM.—Remember that a pint of cream whipped is not a pint of whipped cream. Be careful to notice always whether the recipe calls for whipped cream or cream whipped.

COOKING OF VEGETABLES.—A small scrubbing-brush, which may be bought for five cents, and two small pointed knives for preparing vegetables, should be found in every kitchen. Vegetables should be washed in cold water, and cooked until soft in boiling salted water; if cooked in an uncovered vessel, their color is better kept. For peas and beans add salt to water last half hour of cooking. Time for cooking the same vegetables varies according to freshness and age, therefore time-tables for cooking serve only as guides.

THE FOLLOWING VEGETABLES SHOULD BE COOKED IN BOILING SALTED WATER.—Beets, string beans, brussel sprouts, cabbage, corn, peas, spinach and potatoes, after soaking potatoes in cold water.

Some flour requires more liquid to moisten than others, so your judgement must guide you in bread-making or pastry. Winter wheat flour requires less water than spring wheat flour.

IN SETTING-bread to rise, be careful to place it where it is not too hot or too cool.

WHERE a recipe calls for a cup of anything, always use the standard measuring cup.

IN BOILING chicken or sweetbreads put from one to three tablespoons of l e m o n juice in water. This will blanch and make very tender.

To EXTRACT juice from onion, use an old onion; hold firmly in your hand and press the stem end firmly on a grater, pressing hard and turning just a little. Be careful not to grate.

To REMOVE the odor of onions from the hands, crush parsley in the fingers.

COOKING.

BOILING is to cook in boiling water.

STEAMING is cooking over boiling water.

STEWING is cooking in a small amount of water for a long time. It is the most economical way of cooking meats as all nutriment is retained.

BROILING is cooking over a clear fire.

ROASTING is cooking before a clear fire with reflector to concentrate heat.

BAKING is cooking in an oven.

FRYING is cooking by means of immersion in deep fat. SAUTEING is frying in a small quantity of fat.

Correct measurements are absolutely necessary to insure good results.

A cupful is measured level.

A tablespoonful is measured level.

A teaspoonful is measured level.

A cupful of liquid is all the cup will hold.

Measure butter or lard solidly into cup or spoon and pack level with knife.

FRYING.

Use stale bread grated or put through meat grinder or rolled and sifted. Break egg and beat enough to blend white and yellow and dilute with two tablespoons of water. Roll food to be fried in crumbs, egg and then crumbs again and immerse in hot fat.

TEST FAT FOR FRYING. When fat begins to smoke, drop into it a cube of soft bread and if in forty seconds, it is a golden brown, the fat is right temperature for frying any uncooked mixture. Use same test for uncooked mixtures.

All fried food, when removed from stove should be drained on manila paper.

Be careful not to put too much into frying pan at same time. It lowers temperature of fat. Many kinds of food may be fried in -s a m e fat. New fat should be used for dough mixtures, potatoes, fish and oysters.

TO CLARIFY FAT.—Melt fat, add raw potato cut up and allow fat to heat gradually. When fat stops bubbling and potatoes are well browned, strain through double cheese cloth, placed over wire strainer.

BREAD

POTATO ROLLS.

1 cup of flour.	1 cup potatoes (which have been
¾ cup of lard.	put through a potato-ricer).
1 cup of milk.	2 eggs, well beaten.
½ cup of sugar (scant).	1 teaspoonful of salt.

1 cake of Fleischmann's Compressed Yeast, dissolved in 2 cups of lukewarm water.

Mix thoroughly the lard, potatoes, sugar and salt; add the eggs, then the milk, and then the yeast. Set to rise for two hours; make into a soft dough, by adding about a quart of flour, and set to rise again. Make into rolls or loaf, butter the top, and set to rise again; bake in a quick oven.

PLAIN ROLLS.

1 pint of milk.	2 tablespoonfuls of butter.
2 tablespoonfuls of sugar.	1 teaspoonful of salt.
3 cups of flour for sponge.	¼ cup of lukewarm water.

¼ cake of Fleischmann's Compressed Yeast.

Scald the milk and pour it over the butter, sugar and salt. When cold, add the yeast cake, dissolved in the lukewarm water, then add the flour to make the sponge; beat well; let it r i s e until light. Then add enough flour to knead; knead well—very thoroughly—and set to rise. When light, cut it down, shape into rolls, let it rise again, and bake r a quick oven.

PARKER HOUSE ROLLS.

2 cups scalded milk.	1 teaspoon salt.
3 tablespoons butter.	1 yeast cake dissolved in ¼ cup
2 tablespoons sugar.	lukewarm water.

Flour.

Add butter, sugar and salt to milk; when lukewarm, add dissolved yeast cake and three cups of flour. Beat thoroughly, cover, and let rise until light; cut down, and add enough flour to knead (it will take about two and one half cups). Let rise again, toss on slightly floured board, knead pat, and roll out to one-third inch thickness. Shape with biscuit-cutter, first dipped in flour. Dip the handle of a case knife in flour, and with it make a crease through the middle of each piece; brush over one-half of each piece with melted butter, fold, and press edges together. Place in greased pan, one inch apart, cover, let rise, and bake in hot oven twelve to fifteen minutes. As rolls rise they will part slightly, and if hastened in rising are apt to lose their shape.

ENTIRE WHEAT BREAD.

2 cups scalded milk.	1 teaspoon salt.
¼ cup sugar, or	1 yeast cake dissolved in ¼ cup
⅛ cup molasses.	lukewarm water.

4⅔ cup coarse entire wheat flour.

Add sweetening and salt to milk; cool, and when lukewarm, add dissolved yeast cake and flour; beat well, cover' and let rise to double its bulk. Again beat, and turn into greased bread pans, having pans one-half full; let rise, and bake. Entire wheat bread should not quite double its bulk during last rising. This mixture may be baked in Gem pans.

BOSTON BROWN BREAD

1 cup rye meal.   ¾ tablespoon soda
1 cup granulated corn meal   1 teaspoon salt
1 cup Graham flour.   ¾ cup molasses
     2 cups sour milk, or 1¾ cups sweet milk or water.

Mix and sift dry ingredients, add molasses and milk
stir until well mixed, turn into a well-buttered mould and
steam three and one-half hours. The cover should be buttered before being placed on mould, and then tied down
with string; otherwise the bread in rising might force off
cover. Mould should never be filled more than two-thirds
full. A melon-mould or one-pound baking-powder boxes
make the most attractive-shaped loaves, but a five-pound
lard pail answers the purpose. For steaming, place mould
on a trivet in kettle containing boiling water, allowing water to come half-way up around mould, cover
closely, and steam, adding, as needed, more boiling water
                                              Miss Farmer.

BUNS.

1 cup scalded milk.   ½ teaspoon salt.
⅛ cup butter.   ½ cup raisins stoned and
⅛ cup sugar.   quarters.
1 yeast cake dissolved in   1 teaspoon extract lemon.
¼ cup lukewarm water.   Flour, cinnamon.

Add one-half sugar and salt to milk; when lukewarm,
add dissolved yeast cake and one and one-half cups flour;
cover, and let rise until light; add butter, remaining sugar
raisins, lemon, and flour to make a dough; let rise, shape
like biscuits, let rise again, and bake. If wanted glazed,
brush over with beaten egg before baking

GRAHAM BREAD.

4 cups Graham flour.	1 teaspoon salt.
4 cups white flour.	4 tablespoons of dark molasses
1 cup sugar.	1 qt. buttermilk.

Three-fourths cup of buttermilk with two rounded teaspoons of soda and one teaspoonful of baking powder dissolved and stirred in last.

Grease pans—bake in slow oven one hour.

SALLY LUNN.

One pint of cream, four eggs beaten as for cake separately. Add to the cream one pint of sifted flour and the yolks of the eggs—also a piece of butter (the size of an egg) melted. Then add the whites, and a level teaspoonful of soda dissolved in a little milk. Grease your pans well. Bake and cut in two. Put melted butter between and serve.

DIXIE BISCUITS.

Three pints of flour, one teaspoonful of salt, melt two tablespoonsful of lard in one cup of milk and pour over two eggs well beaten. Put into the flour, then add one cup of yeast. Mix and set to rise about eleven o'clock in winter and twelve o'clock in summer. About five o'clock roll out with just enough flour to prevent sticking. Cut in two sizes. Put small one on top of large one. Put in pan to rise. Bake in quick oven.

BAKING POWDER BISCUIT.

2 cups flour.	1 tablespoon lard.
4 teaspoons baking powder.	¾ cup milk and water in equal
1 teaspoon salt.	parts.
1 tablespoon butter.	

Mix dry ingredients and sift twice.

Work in butter and lard with tips of fingers; add gradually the liquid, mixing with knife to a soft dough. It is impossible to determine the exact amount of liquid, owing to differences in flour. Toss on a floured board, pat, and roll lightly to one-half inch in thickness. Shape with a biscuit-cutter. Place on buttered pan, and bake in hot oven twelve to fifteen minutes. If baked in too slow an oven, the gas will escape before it has done its work.

BEATEN BISCUIT.

1 quart of flour.	¼ cup of lard.
1 cup of cold water.	½ teaspoonful of salt.

Add two tablespoonfuls of m i l k with the water (to make them brown nicely). Rub the lard well into the flour, and add the milky water until you have a stiff dough. Work through a biscuit machine, or beat with an iron until the dough is smooth and light. Bake in a moderate oven.

CORN MUFFINS.

1 pint of meal.	½ pint of milk.
1 tablespoonful of lard.	2 eggs.
1 heaping teaspoon of baking powder	½ teaspoon of salt.

Beat the eggs separately until very light. Then add to the yolks the meal, baking powder, and salt sifted together. Then the lard melted, then the milk, and when just ready to pour into the hot buttered rings, add the whites of eggs beaten to a stiff, dry froth.

WAFFLES.

2 cups of flour.	1 teaspoonful of baking powder
½ teaspoon of salt.	(heaping).
2 eggs, well beaten.	1 ½ tablespoonfuls melted butter.
	1 cup milk.

Mix the flour, baking powder and salt, and sift; then add the well-beaten yolks of two eggs, to which has been added the milk, and stir into the dry mixture. Add the melted butter, then the whites of the two eggs, beaten to a stiff froth. Then have the waffle irons very hot and well greased—pouring off any extra grease, leaving only enough to keep batter from sticking.

BUCKWHEAT CAKES.

⅛ cup fine bread crumbs or meal.   ¼ yeast cake.
2 cups scalded milk.   ½ cup lukewarm water.
½ teaspoon salt.   1 ¾ cups buckwheat flour.
1 tablespoon molasses.

Pour milk over crumbs, and soak thirty minutes; add salt, yeast cake dissolved in lukewarm water, and buckwheat to make a batter thin enough to pour. Let rise over night; in the morning, stir well, add molasses, one-fourth teaspoon soda dissolved in one-fourth cup lukewarm water, and cook as griddle-cakes. Save enough batter to raise another mixing, instead of using yeast cake; it wil require one-half cup.

SOFT CORN BREAD (Spoon Bread).

1½ pints of sweet milk.   ¾ pint of meal.
1 egg.   Salt.
1 teaspoonful of quick yeast.

Bake in oven.

VIRGINIA GRITS BREAD.

Take about two cups of grits, boil it and while hot mix with it, one heaping tablespoon of butter. Beat four eggs very light and stir into the grits. Add one pint of milk, and stir in gradually, and last one-half pint of corn meal. Bake in a deep pan with plenty of heat at the bottom of the oven. Salt to taste. The batter should be about as thick as pound cake batter. If it is thicker than that, add a little more milk.

CORN DODGERS.

1 quart fine cornmeal.	1 teaspoon of salt.
1 teaspoonful baking powder.	2 tablespoons of lard.
1 pint of sweet milk.	

Mix meal, baking powder and salt, then add lard and then milk. Bake in a hot oven and serve.

LUNCHEON ROLLS.

½ cup scalded milk.	2 tablespoons melted butter.
2 tablespoons sugar.	1 egg.
¼ teaspoon salt.	Flour.
½ yeast cake dissolved in 2 tablespoons lukewarm water.	

Add sugar and salt to milk; when lukewarm, add dissolved yeast cake and three-fourths cup flour. Cover and let rise; then add butter, egg well beaten, and enough flour to knead. Let rise again, roll to one half inch thickness, shape with small biscuit-cutter, place in buttered pan close together, let rise again, and bake.

SOUR MILK GRIDDLE-CAKES.

2½ cups flour.	2 cups sour milk.
½ teaspoon salt.	1¼ teaspoons soda.
	1 egg.

Mix and sift flour, salt and soda; add sour milk, and egg well beaten. Drop by spoonfuls on a greased hot griddle; cook on one side. When puffed, full of bubbles, and cooked on edges, turn, and cook other side. Serve with butter and maple syrup.

SWEET MILK GRIDDLE-CAKES.

3 cups flour.	¼ cup sugar.
1½ tablespoons baking powder.	2 cups milk.
1 teaspoon salt.	1 egg.
	2 tablespoons melted butter.

Mix and sift dry ingredients; beat egg, add milk, and pour slowly on first mixture. Beat thoroughly, and add butter. Cook as Sour Milk Griddle Cakes.

ENTIRE WHEAT GRIDDLE-CAKES.

½ cup entire wheat flour.	3 tablespoons sugar.
1 cup flour.	1 egg.
3 teaspoons baking powder.	1¼ cups milk.
½ teaspoon salt.	1 tablespoon melted butter.

Prepare and cook same as Sweet Milk Griddle Cakes.

SOUPS

BROWN SOUP STOCK.

6 lbs. shin of beef.	1 sprig marjoram.
3 quarts cold water.	2 sprigs parsley.
½ teaspoon peppercorns.	Carrot,
6 cloves.	Turnip,
½ bay leaf.	Onion, } ½ cup each, cut in dice.
3 sprigs thyme.	Celery,
	1 tablespoon salt.

Wipe beef, and cut the lean meat in inch cubes. Brown one-third of meat in hot frying-pan in marrow from a marrow bone. Put remaining two-thirds with bone and fat in soup kettle, add water, and let stand for thirty minutes. Place on back of range, add browned meat, and heat gradually to boiling point. As scum rises it should be removed. Cover and cook slowly six hours, keeping below boiling point during cooking. Add vegetables and seasonings, cook one and one-half hours, strain, and cool as quickly as possible.

JULIENNE SOUP.

To one quart clear brown soup stock add one-fourth cup each carrot and turnip, cut in thin strips one and one-half inches long, previously cooked in boiling salted water, and two tablespoons each cooked peas and string beans. Heat to boiling point.

CONSOMME.

2 lbs. lean beef (from the round).	1 small chicken.
2 ounces lean ham.	1 small onion.
2 sprigs parsley.	¼ small carrot.
2 bay leaves.	2 stalks celery.
6 cloves.	2 eggs.
½ lemon (juice of same).	A little celery salt.

Wipe and cut the beef into small pieces; cut the chicken as for fricasseed chicken. Cover with cold water, and stand on the back of the stove where it will slowly heat. Simmer gently for four hours. Fry out a slice of bacon, add the ham cut in dice, the onion and carrot sliced, saute to a delicate brown in two tablespoonfuls of butter; then add this to the stock with the remainder of the vegetables (cutting the celery in pieces) and a little thyme. Let the soup simmer for another hour, strain and stand away to cool. When cold, carefully remove the fat from the surface; put in a kettle over the fire, add the whites and shells of two eggs beaten lightly, two tablespoons of cold water, a little celery salt, and the juice of half a lemon. Let it boil for five minutes, take from the fire and skim carefully, and strain through a cloth. When ready to serve, heat again and season with salt and pepper to taste. The soup should be perfectly clear, but amber in color.

QUICK BOUILLON.

1 tablespoon of butter.	½ small onion, sliced.
1½ lb. of lean chopped beef.	1 stalk of celery.
(round being best).	½ chicken (bones well broken).
4 cloves.	2 sliced carrots.
1 bay leaf.	2 sprigs of parsley.
1½ pints cold water.	1 egg (white and shell).

Melt the butter and add the onion. Cook until the onion is thoroughly done, then add the beef (that from the round being best) and chicken, celery, cloves, carrot, bay leaf, parsley, and cold water. Cover the saucepan and set on the back of the stove wheie the water will slowly heat. Let it come to a boiling point, strain, and return to saucepan and bring to a boil. Beat the white of one egg in one-half cup of water until thoroughly blended, crush the shell and add to the egg and water, and then to the boiling bouillon. Boil four minutes, let it stand one minute to settle, and strain through cheesecloth wrung out of cold water.

ST. GERMAIN.

1 can peas.	Water as much as there is liquor
½ onion.	in the can.
Sprig of parsley.	A blade of mace.
½ teaspoonful of sugar.	1 teaspoonful salt.
½ teaspoonful of pepper.	3 cupfuls brown stock.
A bit of bay leaf.	

Drain and mash the peas, add the water, reserving one-half cup of the peas, putting the remainder into the stew pan with the onion, bay leaf, parsley, mace, sugar, salt and pepper; simmer gently for half an hour, mash thoroughly, and add the hot brown stock. Let it come to the boiling point and rub through a sieve. Thicken with one tablespoonful of butter and one heaping tablespoonful of flour. Cook ten minutes and add the whole peas.—

Miss Farmer.

TOMATO BOUILLON.

Put one can of tomatoes with three pints of brown stock on the fire. Add one tablespoonful of chopped onion, two bay leaves, four whole cloves, one level teaspoon of celery seed and one-half teaspoonful of pepper. Cover and cook twenty minutes. Strain through a sieve.

Beat slightly the whites of three eggs and add to the tomato. Bring to a boil and boil rapidly for five minutes, strain through two thicknesses of cheesecloth. Reheat, season with two teaspoonfuls of salt and serve with small cubes of toasted bread.

CHICKEN SOUP.

One-half full grown tender chicken cut up; one tea cup of fresh milk. Put one quart of cold water on the chicken and cover it closely and let it boil, one hour. Then add one tablespoonful of rice and boil another hour. If it boils down too much, a d d a little boiling water and the last thing put in the milk and have it boiling. Rub a teaspoonful of flour with one of butter to thicken the soup and season with salt and pepper. Fine for the sick.

GREEN PEA SOUP.

Take three pints of shelled peas, half of a chicken. Put on the fire with three pints of water, a little parsley, salt and pepper and when perfectly done, take them from the stock, strain through a colander and put in the stock again. Melt one-fourth pound of butter, add two table spoons of flour, and add to the soup to thicken. Just before serving, add one-half pint of cream.

OKRA SOUP.

To one gallon of boiling water, add one chicken which has been cut up and fried. Take one and one-half pints of sliced okra, eight or ten tomatoes, one onion, parsley, chop them, season with salt and pepper and fry all together and put in the stock; let come to a good boil and serve with steamed rice.

BLACK BEAN SOUP.

Make stock by boiling one large soup bone. Take out
the bone when cold and remove all grease. Soak over night
one pint of black beans. Next day boil beans until very
well done. Mash through a colander, add to soup
stock and put on to boil. To this add one-half teaspoon
of cloves, one-half teaspoon of cinnamon, one-half teaspoon
of allspice (all ground spices). Fry two large onions in
a little lard and add to the soup and let this all come to a
boil. Then add juice of one lemon and one-half tumbler
of sherry; salt and pepper to taste. When ready to serve
add three hard boiled eggs sliced and one lemon sliced.

BOUILLON.

Cut up one three pound chicken, breaking all the bones;
five pounds of lean beef, eight pints of cold water. Let
come to a boil quickly and skim. Add a few slices of
carrot, fresh celery and an onion and a pod of red pepper.
Let it simmer slowly for five hours until reduced to four
pints. Strain through a towel and serve.

FRENCH OYSTER SOUP.

Wash one quart of oysters by adding one cupful of
cold water to the liquor. Pick over oysters, chop slightly
and heat to boiling point. Strain and reserve the liquor.
Scald one quart milk with a slice of onion and one blade of
mace, melt three tablespoonfuls butter, add three of flour,
then add oysters, liquor and milk, after removing the onion
and mace. Add the beaten yolks of two raw eggs. Salt
and pepper to taste and when all is thoroughly blended,
serve.

CORN SOUP.

One-half gallon of milk put on to boil. Cut one pint of green corn close to the ear, and put on with the milk; when it comes to a boil, add one pint of green corn prepared as for pudding. Add butter as you would for oyster soup, salt and pepper to taste. Let boil until corn tastes done.

ASPARAGUS.

1 quart white stock.	1 level tablespoon of butter.
1 pint cream.	1 heaping teaspoonful flour.

1 can asparagus

Put a little more than a quart of white stock (either chicken or veal broth) on the fire with the asparagus, and let them boil hard for fifteen minutes, then strain, pressing all the substance from the asparagus—reserve the tips of asparagus to serve in puree. Thicken the strained stock with the butter and flour, and just before serving add the cream, salt and pepper.

Celery, peas, etc., can be used in the same way.

WHITE SOUP.

1 chicken.	½ teaspoon salt.
6 blades of mace.	Little cayenne pepper.
8 almonds.	Yolks of 4 eggs.

1 quart of cream or milk.

Take one fat, old chicken and cut up; rub soup kettle with butter, put in chicken with one-half teaspoon salt, little cayenne pepper, six blades of mace; cover well with water, stew slowly until done, skimming well, take breasts and wings, chop fine, steep remainder slowly, put three biscuits to soak in a cup of new milk, add yolks of four hard-boiled eggs, a n d chop fine eight almonds, pound chicken perfectly smooth, add soaked bread and eggs, little at a time, and pound to a smooth paste. Strain liquor from remaining chicken, which should be a full quart, pour by degrees into paste, stirring until well mixed; have boiling less than a quart of new milk or cream, add hot by degrees to the mixture, after which return the whole to the pot and let it simmer only a few minutes. Send to the table, and if not rich enough, add a small piece of butter. If the soup boils too much it will curdle. It should be as thick as rich cream.

SPLIT PEA SOUP.

1 cup dried split peas.	3 tablespoons butter.
2½ quarts cold water.	2 tablespoons flour.
1 pint milk.	1½ teaspoons salt.
½ onion.	⅛ teaspoon pepper.
	2-inch cube fat salt pork.

Pick over peas and soak several hours, drain, add cold water, pork, and onion. Simmer three or four hours, or until soft; rub through a sieve. Add butter and flour cooked together, salt and pepper. Dilute with milk, adding more if necessary. The water in which a ham has been cooked may be used; in such case omit salt.

POTATO SOUP.

3 potatoes.	1½ teaspoons salt.
1 quart milk.	¼ teaspoon celery salt.
2 slices onion.	⅛ teaspoon pepper.
3 tablespoons butter.	Few grains cayenne.
2 tablespoons flour.	1 teaspoon chopped parsley.

Cook potatoes in boiling salted water; when soft, rub through a strainer. Scald milk with onion, remove onion, and add milk slowly to potatoes. Melt half the butter, add dry ingredients, stir until well mixed, then stir into boiling soup; cook one minute, strain, add remaining butter, and sprinkle with parsley.

OYSTER BISQUE.

1 quart of oysters.	4 cups of cream.
1 slice of onion.	2 stalks of celery.
2 blades of mace.	1 sprig of parsley.
A bit of bay leaf.	⅓ cup of butter.
⅓ cup of flour.	Salt and pepper to taste.

Scald the oysters and the liquor, separate them after heating to boiling point, strain liquor through cheesecloth, reheat, and thicken with the butter and flour. Scald the milk with the other ingredients mentioned, remove seasonings, add the milk to the oyster liquor, and then add the oysters. Serve hot with whipped cream on top.

TOMATO PUREE.

1 can tomatoes.	1 pint brown stock.
1 bay leaf.	1 sprig parsley.
1 stalk of celery.	1 teaspoonful of sugar.
1 tablespoonful of butter.	Several slices of onion.

Put the tomatoes into a saucepan with the brown stock, bay leaf, parsley, celery and sugar; simmer thoroughly; put the onion and butter into the saute pan, and when the onion is thoroughly done—but not brown—add a table-spoonful of flour, and put all with the tomatoes; season with salt and pepper. Pass the whole through a fine sieve or strainer—heat again and serve.

OX-TAIL SOUP.

1 small ox-tail.		½ teaspoon salt.
6 cups Brown Stock.		Few grains cayenne.
Carrot	½ cup each, cut in fancy shapes.	¼ cup Madeira wine.
Turnip		1 teaspoon Worcestershire Sauce
Onion	½ cup each, cut in small pieces.	
Celery		1 teaspoon lemon juice.

Cut ox-tail in small pieces, wash, drain, sprinkle with salt and pepper, dredge with flour, and fry in butter ten minutes. Add to Brown Stock, and simmer one hour. Then add vegetables, which have been parboiled twenty minutes; simmer until vegetables are soft, add salt, cayenne, wine, Worcestershire Sauce, and lemon juice.

Miss Farmer.

MULLIGATAWNY SOUP.

5 cups White Stock II.		¼ cup butter.
1 cup tomatoes.		⅓ cup flour.
Onions, cut in slices		
Carrot, cut in cubes	¼ cup each.	Sprig of parsley.
Celery, cut in cubes		Blade of mace.
1 pepper, finely chopped.		2 cloves.
1 cup raw chicken cut in dice.		Salt and pepper.

Cook vegetables and chicken in butter until brown; add flour, mace, cloves, parsley, stock, and tomato, and simmer one hour. Strain, reserve chicken, and rub vegetables through sieve. Add chicken to strained soup, season with salt and pepper, and serve with boiled rice.

CREAM OF MUSHROOM SOUP.

¾ lb. mushrooms.	¼ cup flour.
4 cups White or Brown Stock.	1 cup cream.
1 slice onion, small.	Salt.
¼ cup butter.	Pepper.

2 tablespoons Sauterne.

Chop mushrooms, add to White Stock with onion, cook twenty minutes, and rub through a sieve. Reheat, bind with butter and flour cooked together, then add cream and salt and pepper to taste. Just before serving add wine.

CROUTONS (Duchess Crusts).

Cut stale bread in one-third inch slices and remove crusts. Spread thinly with butter. Cut slices in one-third inch cubes, put in pan and bake until delicately browned, or fry in deep fat.

NOODLES.

1 egg.   ½ teaspoon salt.   Flour.

Beat egg slightly, add salt, and flour enough to make very stiff dough; knead, toss on slightly floured board, and and roll thinly as possible, which may be as thin as paper. Cover with towel, and set aside for twenty minutes; then cut in fancy shapes, using sharp knife or French vegetable cutter; or the thin sheet may be rolled like jelly-roll, cut in slices as thinly as possible, and pieces unrolled. Dry, and when needed cook twenty minutes in boiling salted water; drain, and add to soup.

Noodles may be served as a vegetable.

EGG BALLS.

Yelks 2 hard-boiled eggs.   ⅓ teaspoon salt.
Few grains of cayenne.   ½ teaspoon butter.

Rub yolks through sieve, add seasonings, and moisten with raw egg yolk to make consistency to handle. Shape in small balls, roll in flour, and saute in butter. Serve in brown soup stock, consomme, or mock turtle soup.

PATE A CHOUX.

2½ tablespoons milk   ⅛ teaspoon salt.
½ teaspoon lard.   ¼ cup flour.
½ teaspoon butter.   1 egg.

Heat butter, lard and milk to boiling point, add flour and salt, and stir vigorously. Remove from fire, add egg unbeaten, and stir until well mixed. Cool, and drop small pieces from tip of teaspoon into deep fat. Fry until brown and crisp, and drain on brown paper.

CRACKERS WITH CHEESE.

Arrange zephyrettes or saltines in pan. Sprinkle with grated cheese and bake until cheese is melted.

QUENELLES.

Quenelles are made from any kind of force-meat, shaped in small balls or between tablespoons, making an oval, or by forcing mixture through pastry bag on buttered paper. They are cooked in boiling salted water or stock, and are served as garnish to soups or other dishes; when served with sauce, they are an entree.

ROYAL CUSTARD.

Yolks 3 eggs.   ⅛ teaspoon salt.
1 egg.   Slight grating nutmeg.
½ cup Consomme.   Few grains cayenne.

Beat eggs slightly, add Consomme and seasonings. Pour into a small buttered tin mould, place in pan of hot water, and bake until firm; cool, remove from mould, and cut in fancy shapes. Serve in soup.

SOUFFLED CRACKERS.

Split common crackers, and soak in ice water, to cover, eight minutes. Dot over with butter, and bake in a hot oven until puffed and browned.

FISH

FRIED OYSTERS.

Take large select oysters, wash and drain and wipe. Dip them in the yellow of an egg, diluted with two table-spoonfuls of water, then in bread or cracker crumbs; put in frying basket and fry in deep hot lard.

OYSTERS EN COQUILLE.

2 sets of calf brains.   50 oysters.

Carefully clean the brains and boil in salt water; scald the oysters in their own liquor until the edges curl, and then cut in small pieces. Chop the brains and mix with the oysters. Take two tablespoonfuls of butter and saute a little finely chopped onion in it; add to the brains and oysters a little chopped parsley, celery salt, salt and pepper. Then add one-half cup of cream, two tablespoonfuls of stale bread crumbs.

FRICASSEED OYSTERS WITH MUSHROOMS.

Thirty oysters, one-half cup sliced mushrooms, one tablespoonful butter, one tablespoonful of flour, three gills of cream, one gill of mushroom liquor, yolks of two eggs, season with salt, pepper and a little celery salt. Cook together butter and flour over hot water, add seasoning, cream, and mushroom liquor, and then the egg very slowly or it will curdle. Add oysters and mushrooms, and when the oysters are plump and edges curled, serve at once.

OYSTERS EN BROCHETTE.

Poach lightly one dozen large oysters in their own liquor, dry them on a cloth, and lay them in a deep plate, season with salt, pepper. Cover the oysters with olive oil, run them on small skewers, alternating each with slices of cooked mushrooms, brush them over with melted butter, roll them in bread crumbs and broil them for six or seven minutes turning frequently. These are delicious. They are also very nice alternating the oysters with bacon and cook over a hot fire.

SALMON CREAM.

Take one can of salmon or one pound of fresh salmon or other fish. Remove bones and skin, then rub and pound to a smooth paste. Add twelve almonds chopped fine, one teaspoonful of onion juice, one teaspoonful of salt, one-half teaspoonful of white pepper. Mix and add gradually, the unbeaten whites of three eggs. Then stir in a half pint of cream whipped to a stiff froth. Fill molds, set in a pan of boiling water and cook in a moderate oven twenty minutes. Turn on a platter and serve with a rich sauce.

MUSHROOM AND OYSTER EN COQUILLE.

Parboil one pint of oysters; drain; reserve the liquor and add milk to make a cup full. Melt one and one-half tablespoonfuls of butter; àdd one and one-half tablespoonfuls of flour and brown; add the oyster liquor and the oysters, and one-third cupful of canned mushrooms cut in quarters; 1 teaspoonful of anchovy essence, a few grains of cayenne and salt to taste.

PANNED OYSTERS.

Clean one pint large oysters. Place in dripping-pan small oblong pieces of toast, put an oyster on each piece, sprinkle with salt and pepper, and bake until oysters are plump. Serve with lemon butter.

Lemon Butter. Cream three tablespoons butter, add one-half teaspoon salt, one tablespoon lemon juice, and a few grains cayenne.

SCALLOPED OYSTERS.

1 pint oysters.	1 cup cracker crumbs.
4 tablespoons oyster liquor.	½ cup melted butter.
2 tablespoons milk or cream.	Salt.
½ cup stale bread crumbs.	Pepper.

Mix bread and cracker crumbs, and stir in butter. Put a thin layer in bottom of a buttered shallow baking-dish, cover with oysters, and sprinkle with salt and pepper; add one-half each oyster liquor and cream. Repeat, and cover top with remaining crumbs. Bake thirty minutes in hot oven. Never allow more than two layers of oysters for Scalloped Oysters; if three layers are used, the middle layer will be underdone, while others are properly cooked. A sprinkling of mace or grated nutmeg to each layer is considered by many an improvement. Sherry wine may be used in place of cream.

SAVORY OYSTERS.

1 pint of oysters.	½ cup Brown Stock.
4 tablespoons butter.	1 teaspoon Worcestershire Sauce.
4 tablespoons flour.	Few drops onion juice.
1 cup oyster liquor.	Salt.
	Pepper.

Clean oysters, parboil and drain. Melt butter, add flour and stir until well browned. Pour on gradually, while stirring constantly, oyster liquor and stock. Add seasonings and oysters. Serve on toast, in timbale cases, patty shells, or vol-au-vents.

SAUTED OYSTERS.

Clean one pint oysters, sprinkle on both sides with salt and pepper. Take up by the tough muscle with plated fork and dip in cracker crumbs. Put two tablespoons butter in hot frying-pan, add oysters, brown on one side, then turn and brown on the other.

OYSTER PATTIE FILLING.

1 tablespoon of butter.	½ cup oyster liquor.
2 tablespoons of flour.	½ teaspoon of lemon juice.
½ cup cream.	Salt and pepper to taste.

Scald 1 pint of oysters in liquor, melt butter, add flour then cream and oyster liquor, salt, pepper and lemon juice. Stir until it thickens then add oysters and serve in pattie shells or Croutades. If chicken, sweetbreads or mushrooms are used instead of oysters, substitute white stock for oyster liquor or use 1 cup of cream.

OYSTER RAREBIT.

6 oysters.	½ lb. of cheese.
2 eggs.	Salt spoon of salt.
1 tablespoon butter.	Salt spoon of mustard.
	Salt spoon of cayenne pepper.

Clean and remove the muscle from one-half pint of oysters. Parboil them in a chafing dish in their own liquor until the edges curl. Remove to a hot bowl. Put one tablespoonful of butter, one-half pound of cheese, broken in small pieces, one salt spoon each of salt, mustard, and a few grains of cayenne pepper into the chafing dish. While the cheese is melting beat two eggs slightly and add to them the oyster liquor. Mix this gradually with the melted cheese, add the oysters, and turn out and serve over hot toast.

OYSTERS A LA NEWBURG.

25 oysters.	Salt spoon of salt.
Heaping tablespoon butter.	Yolk of 1 egg.
½ salt spoon of pepper.	4 spoons of milk or cream.
2 teaspoons of sherry.	

Into a pan which is very hot throw your oysters first having drained all the liquor from them. To twenty-five oysters allow a piece of butter the size of a walnut, pepper and salt. Stir until your oysters curl. Then quickly add the beaten yolk of an egg, to which has been added the milk or cream. After these are thoroughly mixed, add two teaspoonfuls of sherry; stir well, but do not allow the mixture to come to a boil. Serve on squares of toast.

OYSTER COCKTAIL.

Put six tablespoons of tomato catsup, three tablespoons of Tarragon vinegar, three teaspoons of Worcestershire sauce, three drops of tabasco, eight small oysters in each glass, and on top of all sprinkle a teaspoonful of very finely chopped celery.

BROILED LIVE LOBSTER.

Live lobsters may be dressed for broiling at market, or may be done at home. Clean lobster and place in a buttered wire broiler. Broil eight minutes on flesh side, turn and broil six minutes on shell side. Serve with melted butter. Lobsters taste nearly the same placed in dripping pan and baked fifteen minutes in hot oven, and are much easier cooked.

TO SPLIT A LIVE LOBSTER.

Cross large claws and hold firmly with left hand. With sharp-pointed knife, held in right hand, begin at the mouth and make a deep incision, and, with a sharp cut, draw the knife quickly through body and entire length of tail. Open lobster, remove intestinal vein, liver and stomach, and crack claw shells with a mallet.

SALPICON OF LOBSTER.

Put one level tablespoon of butter in double boiler. Add one tablespoon of flour, then one-quarter cup of cream, and one-quarter cup of white stock; season with salt and cayenne, and when it thickens, add one tablespoon of chopped lobster, six mushrooms chopped fine, and one small truffle chopped fine. Serve in lobster claws or shells.

STUFFED LOBSTER.

Two pounds of lobster, one and one-half cups of cream and rich white stock, bit of bay leaf, three tablespoons of butter, three tablespoons of flour, yolks of two eggs, one teaspoon of lemon juice, one teaspoon of chopped parsley. Season with salt, cayenne, and a little grated nutmeg. Scald stock with bay leaf and remove bay leaf. Melt butter, add flour, then stock and seasonings, then yolks slightly beaten, and the lemon juice. When sauce is thick add lobster and fill the shell. Cover with buttered bread crumbs and brown. Serve in a nest of water cresses.

LOBSTER CUTLETS.

Melt two level tablespoonfuls of butter, add two heaping tablespoonfuls of flour, one teaspoonful of salt, pepper to taste, one-half cup of white stock, and one-half cup of cream. When smooth add one-half teaspoon finely chopped parsley, one beaten egg, and enough chopped lobster, mushrooms and truffles to make one pint. Cook a few minutes and pour out on platter, and let it get thoroughly cold (the colder the better). Shape, dip in bread crumbs, then egg, and then crumbs, and fry in hot fat.

LOBSTER TIMBALS.

2 slices of stale bread.	1 pound halibut or cod.
1 egg, 1 yolk	4 tablespoonfuls of rich cream.
½ tablespoon onion chopped fine.	3 tablespoonfuls of butter.
2 tablespoonfuls of flour.	1 tablespoon sherry wine.
⅔ cup of lobster.	Salt and pepper to taste.

Soak two slices of stale bread in water until soft, squeeze until entirely free from water, cook with a teaspoonful of butter, beating to the consistency of India rubber, then cool; put one pound of halibut or cod through a meat chopper, and then pound in a mortar. Add gradually one-third cup of bread, one egg, one yelk and four tablespoonfuls of rich cream; beat well. Butter timbal molds and spread the bread mixture on sides and bottom; fill with the following lobster filling.

Saute one-half tablespoonful of onion, chopped very fine, in three tablespoonfuls of butter; add two tablespoonfuls of flour, one-half cup of rich cream, yolks of two eggs, salt and pepper to taste. When this thickens, add a tablespoonful of sherry wine and two-thirds of a cup of chopped lobster; pour out to cool, fill the center of the timbals, cover with the fish, and cook in a hot oven in a pan of hot water; serve with lobster sauce. This proportion makes six timbals.

LOBSTER A LA NEWBURG.

1 pint finely chopped lobster.	½ pint cream.
Yolks of 3 eggs.	⅛ glass of sherry.
½ teaspoonful of salt.	A little red pepper.

Put the cream, wine and beaten yolks together in a double boiler and cook, stirring steadily until the sauce thickens. Put in the lobster, let it become heated through, season and serve. A larger portion of sherry may be used if desired. Be very careful to cook this over boiling water, as it curdles very easily.

TOMATOES STUFFED WITH LOBSTER OR FISH.

6 large ripe tomatoes.	1 cup of cream.
1 cup heaping full of lobster or fish.	½ teaspoon salt.
2 tablespoons of butter.	Few grains of pepper.
2 tablespoons of flour.	1 teaspoon lemon juice.

Melt the butter; add flour, and when thoroughly blended add the cream and seasonings. Cook until thick; then add the lobster meat or fish which has been cooked previously. Without peeling the tomatoes, scoop out the tops and fill with creamed fish or lobster. Put in hot oven, and cook until tomatoes are thoroughly done. Then serve with allemande, bechamel or mushroom sauce.

SOFT-SHELL CRABS.

Clean crabs, sprinkle with salt and pepper, dip in crumbs, egg and crumbs, fry in deep fat, and drain. Being light, they will rise to top of fat, and should be turned while frying.

TO CLEAN A CRAB.

Lift and fold back the tapering points which are found on each side of the back shell, and remove spongy sub-

stance that lies under them. Turn crab on its back, and
with a pointed knife remove the small piece at lower part
of shell, which terminates in a point: this is called
the apron.

TO BROIL A CRAB (Soft Shell).

Clean crab, sprinkle with salt and pepper, dredge witų
ou r and broil in butter. Garnish with water cress and
lemon and serve with or without tartar sauce.

TARTAR SAUCE.

One-half cup of mayonnaise dressing (No. 1); add one
teaspoon onion juice, a dessertspoon chopped capers, one
teaspoon chopped pickle.

DEVILED CRABS (Hard Shell).

2 dozen crabs.	½ teaspoon mustard.
1 egg.	1 teaspoon thyme.
½ teaspoon salt.	Ground cloves, allspice and parsley
Little black or red pepper.	1 tablespoon olive oil.
1 level tablespoon butter.	1 teaspoon of chopped onions.

Boil two dozen crabs twenty minutes with a little salt,
then remove meat, reserving the number of empty shells
needed. The meat from two dozen crabs will fill nine
shells. Cut the crab meat fine, mix it well with one raw
(beaten) egg and the pepper, mustard, cloves, allspice,
parsley and thyme; add the olive oil, butter and chopped
onion. Let all stand a short time in a bowl until the meat
is seasoned, stuff the empty shells, place them in a pan for
baking, cover them with another raw beaten egg, mix with
fine salted bread crumbs; bake in oven about fifteen minutes.

TO BROIL FISH.

Clean and wipe fish dry as possible, sprinkle with salt and pepper, and place in a well-greased wire broiler. Slices of fish should be turned often while broiling. Pompano, blue fish and mackerel are split down the back and broiled whole, removing tail and head or not, as desired. Whole fish should be first broiled on flesh side and then turned and broiled on skin side, just long enough to make skin brown and crisp. To broil sliced fish, such as salmon, halibut, white fish or trout, cut in two inch slices, and should be turned often while broiling.

BAKED RED SNAPPER.

Clean a four-pound red snapper, sprinkle the inside with salt and pepper, and stuff and sew together or pin together. Place in a greased pan, and if you have no fish sheet, fold in cheesecloth, bake in hot oven for about three-quarters of an hour or until thoroughly done, basting frequently. Serve with hollandaise sauce or plain white sauce.

STUFFING FOR FISH.

½ cup cracker crumbs.	½ teaspoon salt.
½ cup stale bread crumbs.	⅛ tablespoon pepper.
¼ cup melted butter.	½ cup of hot water.

Few drops of onion juice.

Mix ingredients in order given.

TO COOK FISH IN BOILING WATER.

Small cod, haddock or cusk are cooked whole in enough boiling water to cover, to which is added salt and lemon juice or vinegar. Salt gives flavor; lemon juice or vinegar keeps the flesh white. A long fish-kettle containing a rack on which to place fish is useful but rather expensive. In place of fish-kettle, if the fish is not too large to be coiled in it, a frying-basket may be used placed in any kettle. The fish is cooked when flesh leaves the bone, no matter how long the time.

FISH PUDDING.*

1 pound boiled fish.	½ cup of cream.
1½ tablespoons of flour.	1½ teaspoons of salt
¼ teaspoonful of pepper.	1 teaspoonful lemon juice.
A little onion juice.	2 eggs.

Mash the fish thoroughly, then put through a puree sieve and add seasonings. Put butter in the saucepan, and when melted add the flour, then the cream, then the beaten eggs, stirring until well scalded, not thick. Then add the fish, beat well and fill a ring mold with the pudding, pressing it well against the sides; set the whole in a pan of water and put in a moderate oven for thirty minutes. Remove on to a dish, and fill in the center with Parisienne potatoes, making a border of the same outside, and serve with rich cream sauce, in which parsley is chopped.—*Century Cook Cook.*

FISH CROQUETTES.

1 pint boiled fish.	½ teaspoonful of onion juice.
½ teaspoonful pepper.	1 tablespoonful of butter.
1 cupful of cream.	Yolks of two eggs and a little
2 tablespoonfuls of flour.	chopped parsley.
1 teaspoonful salt.	

Put the butter into a saucepan; when melted add the flour, and when thoroughly mixed add the cream, then the seasonings, then the beaten yolks of two eggs, and then

---

*If a dry fish, such as halibut or haddock, is used, slash body at intervals and insert thin slices of fat pork; in other words, lard it.

the fish and the parsley. Spread on a dish to cool; make out into croquettes; to the beaten yolk of one egg add two tablespoonfuls of water. Dip the croquettes first into the stale bread crumbs, then in egg, and then in crumbs. Fry in boiling fat. Serve with either bechamel or hollandaise sauce.

BROILED SHAD ROE.

Wash and dry the roe, then broil them very slowly and keep them moistened with butter to prevent the skin from breaking. They may also be cooked by sauteing in butter. Cook them brown, cover the top with butter, pepper, salt and a little lemon juice and sprinkle with chopped parsley. Garnish with lemon and water cress, and serve some of the water cress with each portion. Serve with maitre d'hotel butter.

MEATS

VEAL CROQUETTES.

3 pounds of veal.	2 eggs.
1 loaf of bread.	1 teaspoonful of onions.
¼ pound of butter.	1 teaspoonful of parsley.
1 nutmeg.	¼ pound calf brains.

Boil the veal and when cold, grind in a meat grinder. Put boiling water on bread and beat into this one egg. Stir on the fire until it is like mush and set to cool. Add this to the veal, and season with the chopped parsley and onion and add the other egg. Mix thoroughly. Add two tablespoonfuls of cream and the brains which have been parboiled. Roll into croquettes, dip in crumbs, egg and crumbs and fry in hot fat.

DELICIOUS LUNCHEON DISH.

One and one-half pounds cold roast or braised beef, three ounces of broiled fresh mushrooms, three ounces of cooked potatoes, all cut in small pieces; also one ounce of cold boiled ham cut in small pieces. Fry one ounce of chopped small onion (if desired) in one tablespoon of butter, then add the meat, potatoes, etc. Take one tablespoonful of butter, melt and add one tablespoonful of flour, and then one-half cup of brown sauce, one-half cup tomato puree and when it begins to thicken pour over the other ingredients. Let it get very hot but not boil. Serve on a platter with slices of bread fried in batter or with toast and bunches of parsley.

VEAL CUTLETS.

Trim the cutlets and season with salt and pepper. Dip in bread crumbs, beaten egg and crumbs and fry in smoking hot fat from six to eight minutes. Serve with:

TOMATO SAUCE.

Stew one-half can of tomatoes and one-half small onion together ten minutes. Rub the tomato through a strainer. Cook one tablespoonful of butter and one heaping tablespoonful of flour in a saucepan, add the strained tomatoes and season with one-half teaspoonful of salt and one-eighth teaspoonful of pepper. Stir till it thickens and serve.

BROILED BREADED BEEF.

Cut rare roast beef in pieces three-quarters of an inch thick, sprinkle with salt, pepper and onion juice if desired. Brush over with white of egg beaten slightly, and roll in bread crumbs. Place on a well-greased broiler and broil over a clear fire five minutes.

PRESSED CHICKEN.

1 fat hen.	½ box Cox gelatin.
1 quart water.	1 lemon.
1 dozen eggs.	Salt, pepper and thyme

Boil the hen until very tender, pick from the bones and chop fine. Boil the eggs hard and slice. Dissolve the gelatine in one-half pint of cold water and add to the liquor in which chicken was boiled, making one and one-half pints of liquid. Line bottom of mold with sliced eggs and chicken, alternating, pouring in a little of the liquid with each layer, which should be seasoned with salt, pepper, thyme and juice of one lemon. When all the material is used pour on all the liquid. Put in a cool place to congeal Slice and serve cold.

ROAST BEEF.

The best cuts of beef for roasting are: Tip or middle of sirloin, back of rump, or first three ribs. Tip of sirloin roast is desirable for a small family. Back of rump makes a superior roast for a large family, and is more economical than sirloin. It is especially desirable where a large quantity of dish gravy is liked, for in carving the meat juices follow the knife. Rib roasts contain more fat than either of the others, and are somewhat cheaper.

To Roast Beef.

Wipe, put on a rack in dripping-pan, skin side down, rub over with salt, and dredge meat and pan with flour. Place in hot oven, that the surface may be quickly seared, thus preventing escape of inner juices. After flour in pan is browned, reduce heat, and baste with fat which has tried out; if meat is quite lean, it may be necessary to put trimmings of fat in pan. Baste every ten minutes; if this rule is followed, meat will be found more juicy.

BROILED LAMB CHOPS-French Style.

Broiled on one side, six French Chops. Place in buttered baking dish, cooked side up and cover with Mushroom Sauce. Bake in hot oven eight minutes and serve.

Mushroom Sauce.

Brown one and one-half tablespoons of butter, add three tablespoons of flour, and stir until well browned, then add one-fourth pound of fresh Mushrooms. When tender add one-half cup highly seasoned, Brown Stock, salt and pepper to taste, cook three minutes and pour over cooked side of lamb chops.

BAKED MEAT DINNER.

One pound flat noodles, one pound round steak, ground fine, one can of tomatoes. Boil noodles twenty minutes in salt water. Fry steak in two tablespoonfuls of butter for ten minutes, place with noodles in baking dish, season highly with Worcester and Paprika and salt after mixing thoroughly, pour tomatoes over top and cook slowly for one hour.

COTTAGE PIE.

Cover bottom of a small greased baking-dish with hot mashed potato, add a thick layer of roast beef, chopped or cut in small pieces (seasoned with salt, pepper, and a few drops onion juice) and moistened with some of the gravy; cover with a thin layer of mashed potato, and bake in a hot oven long enough to heat through.

TO BOIL HAM.

Wash ham thoroughly, place in iron kettle or boiler, cover well with water to which has been added one quart of New Orleans molasses and one pint of best cider vinegar. Boil for four or five hours, let ham stay in water until cold, remove from water, take off outside skin, sprinkle with sugar and fine bread crumbs and stick with cloves. Bake one hour in slow oven.

Any ham cooked in this way tastes like "old country ham."

SLICE OF BAKED HAM.

Slice of ham one inch thick. Two tablespoonsful of dry
One cup of granulated sugar. mustard.

Place ham in small baking pan, sugar on top, then cover with dry mustard, then water about half the depth of ham, bake slowly one and one-half hours.

ROAST FILLET.

The fillet should be plentifully larded and all of the sinewy skin and gristle removed from the top, and most of the fat from the under side.   Then place in a baking pan thin slices of larding or pickled pork, chopped onion, carrot, turnip and celery; then place the fillet on this.   Pour over it a cupful of brown stock, salt and pepper, chopped parsley, bay leaf and cloves.   Cook in a hot oven for thirty minutes, basting frequently.   When done, drain off the gravy and remove grease from the top.   Take a tablespoonful of butter, add a tablespoonful of flour, cook together until they are brown.   Add the gravy and a little brown stock—a cupful in all—stir until it boils, add a canful of mushrooms, chopped, and let it simmer for five minutes; then add a little Madeira or sherry; pour round the fillet and serve.

BROILED FILLETS.

Select small beef tenderloins, two inches thick; lard thoroughly; let them lay for two hours in a strong, highly seasoned stock with two tablespoonfuls of claret; broil for a few minutes over a hot fire; serve with drawn butter or mushroom sauce.

BROILED BEEFSTEAK.

Select porterhouse steak at least one inch thick, wipe off with wet cloth rub over with lemon.   With some of the fat which must be trimmed off, grease wire broiler, and place meat in it.   Broil over hot fire at first, that surface may be well seared, thus preventing escape of juices.   After this, turn occasionally until well cooked on both sides.   Remove to hot platter, spread with butter and sprinkle with salt and pepper.

BEEFSTEAK IN OYSTER BLANKET.

Select a porterhouse steak, at least an inch and a half thick, remove the bone, wipe off with a wet cloth, rub over with lemon. With some of the fat which must be trimmed off, grease the wire broiler and place the meat in it; broil over a very hot fire at first that the surface may be well seared, thus preventing the escape of juices. After this, turn occasionally until cooked on both sides; remove to a baking pan, cover thoroughly with select oysters, placing a little butter here and there all over it. Squeeze the juice of half a lemon and place in a hot oven; cook until the oysters plump and the edges curl; season with salt and pepper. Serve with melted butter, a little lemon juice, and chopped parsley.

HAMBURG STEAKS.

Chop finely one pound lean raw beef; season highly with salt, pepper and a few drops onion juice or one-half shallot finely chopped. Shape, cook and serve as meat cakes. A few gratings of nutmeg and one egg slightly beaten may be added.

LAMB CHOPS A LA MAINTENON.

Wipe six French chops, which should be one and one-half inches thick. Split meat in half, cutting to the bone. Cook two and one-half tablespoons of butter and one tablespoon of chopped onion five minutes. Remove onion, add one-half cup chopped mushrooms and cook five minutes. Add two tablespoons of flour, three tablespoons of brown stock, one teaspoon of finely chopped parsley, and season with salt and pepper. Spread this mixture between the split chops, press the edges well together and broil eight minutes. Serve with melted butter or Spanish sauce.

MINCED LAMB ON TOAST.

Remove dry pieces of skin and gristle from remnants of cold roast lamb, then chop meat. Heat in well buttered frying-pan, season with salt, pepper and celery salt, and moisten with a little hot water or stock; or, after seasoning, dredge well with flour, stir, and add enough stock to make thin gravy. Pour over small slices of buttered toast.

BREADED VEAL CUTLETS.

Leave the cutlet whole, or cut it into pieces of uniform size and shape. Salt and pepper. Dip in egg and cover with bread crumbs or cracker crumbs. Fry in hot lard and serve with tomato or cream sauce.

SCALLOPED LAMB.

Remove skin and fat from thin slices of cold roast lamb and sprinkle with salt and pepper. Cover bottom of baking dish with butter and cracker crumbs, cover crumbs with meat; cover m e a t with boiled macaroni and add another layer of meat and macaroni; pour over tomato sauce and cover with buttered cracker crumbs. Bake in hot oven until crumbs are brown. Cold boiled rice may be used in place of the macaroni.

RAGOUT OF VEAL.

Reheat two cups cold roast veal, cut in cubes, in one and one-half cups brown sauce seasoned with one teaspoon Worcestershire sauce, few drops of onion juice and a few grains of cayenne.

POULTRY AND GAME

BROILED CHICKEN.

After chicken has been cleaned thoroughly, split through the back, wash and wipe well. Put a piece of bacon under each wing and on the broiler, and season well with salt, pepper and butter. Broil twenty minutes over a clear fire, watching carefully and turning broiler so that all parts may be equally browned. The flesh side must be exposed to the fire the greater part of time, as the skin side will brown quickly. Remove to a hot platter, spread with soft butter, and sprinkle with salt and pepper. Chickens are so apt to burn while broiling that many prefer to partially cook in oven. Place chicken in dripping-pan, skin side down, sprinkle with salt and pepper, dot over with butter, and bake fifteen minutes in hot oven; then broil to finish cooking. Put on hot platter and garnish with pastry crullers and parsley.

CHICKEN GUMBO.

Dress, clean and cut up a chicken. Sprinkle with salt and pepper, dredge with flour and saute in pork fat. Fry one-half finely chopped onion in fat remaining in frying pan. Add four cups sliced okra, sprig of parsley and one-fourth red pepper finely chopped, and cook slowly fifteen minutes. Add to chicken, with one and one-half cups tomatoes, three cups boiling water, and one and one-half teaspoons salt. Cook slowly until chicken is tender, then add one cup boiled rice. Serve on toast.

ROAST TURKEY.

Dress, clean, stuff and truss a ten-pound turkey. Place on its side on rack in a dripping-pan, rub entire surface with salt and spread breast, legs and wings with one-third cup butter, rubbed until creamy and mixed with one-fourth cup flour. Dredge bottom of pan with flour. Place in a hot oven, and when flour on turkey begins to brown, reduce heat, baste with fat in pan, and add two cups boiling water. Continue basting every fifteen minutes until turkey is cooked, which will require about three hours. For basting, use one-half cup of butter melted in one-half cup boiling water and after this is used baste with fat in pan. During cooking turn turkey frequently, that it may brown evenly. If turkey is browning too fast, cover with buttered paper to prevent burning. Remove string and skewers before serving. Garnish with parsley or celery tips.

For stuffing, use double the quantities given in recipes under Roast Chicken. If stuffing is to be served cold, add one beaten egg. Turkey is often roasted with chestnut stuffing.

GRAVY.

Pour off liquid in pan in which turkey has been roasted. From liquid skim off six tablespoons fat; return fat to pan and brown with six tablespoons flour; pour on gradually three cups stock in which giblets, neck and tips of wings have been cooked, or use liquor left in pan. Cook five minutes, season with salt and pepper; strain. For giblet gravy, add to the above, giblets (heart, liver and gizzard) finely chopped.

CHESTNUT GRAVY.

To two cups thin turkey gravy add three-fourths cup cooked and mashed chestnuts.

CHESTNUT STUFFING.

3 cups French chestnuts.	⅛ teaspoon pepper.
½ cup butter.	¼ cup cream.
1 teaspoon salt.	1 cup cracker crumbs.

Shell and blanch chestnuts. Cook in boiling salted water until soft. Drain and mash, using a potato ricer. Add one-half the butter, salt, pepper and cream. Melt remaining butter, mix with cracker crumbs, then combine mixtures.

MOCK TERRAPIN.

1½ cups cold cooked chicken or veal cut in dice.	Whites 2 hard-boiled eggs, chopped.
1 cup White Sauce I.	3 tablespoons sherry wine.
Yelks 2 hard-boiled eggs finely chopped.	¼ teaspoon salt.
	Few grains cayenne.

Add to sauce, chicken, yelks and whites of eggs, salt and cayenne; cook two minutes, and add wine.

BROILED QUAIL.

Broil same as chicken. Allow eight minutes for cooking. Serve on toast and garnish with parsley and thin slices of lemon.

ROAST QUAIL.

Dress, clean and stuff the same as chicken, adding pecans or oysters to dressing. Bind with thin slices of bacon and roast from fifteen to twenty minutes and serve with gravy.

GOOD STUFFING FOR TURKEY OR CHICKEN.

Moisten a cupful of bread crumbs with melted butter, season highly with salt, pepper, thyme, chopped parsley, and onion juice. Or, put in a saucepan a tablespoonful of butter and fry in it one onion chopped fine, then add a cupful of bread which has been soaked in water, all of the water having been pressed out thoroughly, one-half cupful of stock, a teaspoonful of salt, a teaspoon each of pepper and thyme, one-half cup of celery cut into very small pieces. Stir it until it leaves the sides of the pan, then stuff either turkey or chicken.—*Century Cook Book.*

VEGETABLES

BOILED POTATOES.

Select potatoes of uniform size. Wash, pare and drop at once in cold water to prevent discoloration; soak one-half hour in the fall, and one to two hours in winter and spring. Cook in boiling salted water until soft, which is easily determined by piercing with a skewer. For seven potatoes allow one tablespoon salt, and boiling water to cover. Drain from water, and keep uncovered in warm place until serving time. Avoid sending to table in a covered vegetable dish. In boiling large potatoes, it often happens that outside is soft, while center is underdone. To finish cooking without potatoes breaking apart add one pint cold water, which drives heat to center, thus accomplishing the cooking.

MASHED POTATOES.

To five riced potatoes add three tablespoons butter, one teaspoon salt, few grains pepper, and one-third cup hot milk; beat with fork until creamy, reheat and pile lightly in hot dish.

DUCHESS POTATOES.

To two cups hot riced potatoes add two tablespoons butter, one-half teaspoon salt and yolks of three eggs slightly beaten. Shape (using pastry bag and tube) in form of baskets, pyramids, crowns, leaves, roses, etc. Brush over with beaten egg diluted with one teaspoon water, and brown in a hot oven.

POTATOES EN SURPRISE.

Season one pint of hot mashed potatoes with one table-spoonful of butter, one teaspoonful of salt, one-fourth teaspoonful of celery salt, one-fourth teaspoonful of pepper, and a few grains of cayenne. Add six drops of onion juice, cool slightly, and then add yelk of one egg beaten slightly. Shape into balls. Make a hole in the center, fill with creamed chicken, oysters or sweetbreads. Close up, dip in crumbs, diluted egg and crumbs, and place in a frying-basket and fry in hot fat. Serve with cream or oyster sauce.

POTATO CROQUETTES.

2 cups hot riced potatoes.	¼ teaspoon celery salt.
2 tablespoons butter.	Few grains cayenne.
½ teaspoon salt.	Few drops onion juice.
⅛ teaspoon pepper.	Yelk 1 egg.

1 teaspoon finely chopped parsley

Mix ingredients in order given and beat thoroughly. Shape, dip in crumbs, egg and crumbs again, fry one minute in deep fat and drain on brown paper. Croquettes are shaped in a variety of forms. The most common way is to first form a smooth ball by rolling one rounding tablespoon mixture between hands. Then roll on a board until of desired length and flatten ends.

FRENCH FRIED POTATOES.

Wash and pare small potatoes, cut in eighths, lengthwise, and soak one hour in cold water. Take from water, dry between towels and fry in deep fat. Drain on brown paper and sprinkle with salt. Care must be taken that fat is not too hot, as potatoes must be cooked as well as browned.

SOUBRICS OF SPINACH.

Cook two quarts spinach, drain thoroughly and chop. Add two tablespoons grated Parmesan cheese and two egg-yelks. Season with salt, cayenne and nutmeg and cook eight minutes; then add the white of one egg. Measure by rounding tablespoonfuls, saute in butter and serve with white or cream sauce.

SPAGHETTI A LA KING HUMBERT.

1 quart can tomatoes.	3 pound fat chicken.
⅔ tea cup Italian olive oil.	10 cents worth parmesan cheese
1 large can French mushrooms.	grated.
	1 package spaghetti.

Boil chicken until it is tender (save the chicken liquor). Cut chicken up into dice. Break spaghetti into small pieces. Into bottom of large baking dish, put one layer of spaghetti, one of tomatoes, one of mushrooms, one of grated cheese, one of chicken. Over this pour a small quantity of oil. Proceed in like manner, with alternating layers, until ingredients are used or pan is full, then pour over all slowly the chicken liquor. Bake in slow oven for one hour.

TOMATO WITH EGGS.

Take firm, ripe tomatoes. Scoop out the blossom end, chop up the tomato, cold boiled beef, chicken or lamb together, season well and stir in butter or milk and line the tomato. Drop in a raw egg and place tomatoes in a pan. Place in moderate oven and bake until white of egg cooks Baste constantly with butter, and when ready to serve chop parsley on top. Serve on buttered toast.

HOMINY AND HORSERADISH CROQUETTES.

Steam one-half cup of hominy in three-quarters cup of boiling water until hominy has absorbed water. Add one-half teaspoon salt and three-quarters cup scalded milk and cook until tender. Add two tablespoons butter and four teaspoons of grated horseradish. Shape, dip in crumbs, egg and crumbs. Fry in deep, hot fat. Fine with meat course.

CORN PUDDING.

Take five well filled ears of corn; cut the grain through the center, the whole length of the cob, and by pressing on it with the dull edge of the knife, the interior of the grain will be removed leaving the skin. Into this put two eggs, one-half teaspoonful of salt, one-half teaspoonful of sugar and one-half teaspoonful of baking powder one tablespoonful of melted butter and one-quarter glass of milk or cream. Stir all together until light, put in a baking dish and bake for 15 or 20 minutes in slow oven. This serves five.

HASHED BROWN POTATOES.

Try out fat salt pork cut in small cubes; remove scraps; there should be about one-third cup of fat. Add two cups cold boiled potatoes finely chopped, one-eight teaspoon pepper, and salt if needed. Mix potatoes thoroughly with fat; cook three minutes, stirring constantly let stand to brown underneath. Fold as an omelet and turn on hot platter.

PARISIENNE POTATOES.

With a French vegetable cutter, cut potato balls out of peeled raw potatoes. Drop in cold water for about half an hour. Put into boiling salted water and boil about fif-

teen minutes or until tender. Drain off the water and
let stand on the back of range, covered over, until dry.
Serve with white sauce and chopped parsley.

STUFFED SWEET POTATOES.

Select good, firm sweet potatoes. Wash well and boil
until tender, remove from fire, cut in half, take out most
of the potato, leaving the skin firm enough to stuff. Mash
potato well, season with butter, cream, a little sugar and
cinnamon and sherry wine to taste. Fill shells with potatoes and put in oven to brown a little.

GLAZED SWEET POTATOES.

Wash and pare six medium-sized potatoes. Cook ten
minutes in boiling salted water. Drain, cut in halves
lengthwise, and put in a buttered pan. Make a syrup by
boiling three minutes one-half cup sugar and four tablespoons water. Add one tablespoon butter. Brush potatoes with syrup and bake fifteen minutes, basting twice
with remaining syrup.

SWEET POTATOES EN BROCHETTE.

Wash and pare potatoes and cut in one-third inch
slices. Arrange on skewers in groups of three or four;
parboil six minutes, and drain. Brush over with melted
butter, sprinkle with brown sugar, and bake in a hot oven
until well browned.

SWEET POTATO CROQUETTES.

To two cups hot riced sweet potatoes add three tablespoons butter, one half-teaspoon salt, few grains pepper,

and one beaten egg. Shape in croquettes, dip in crumbs, egg, and crumbs again, fry in deep fat, and drain. If potatoes are very dry, it will be necessary to add hot milk to moisten.

BROILED TOMATOES.

Wipe and cut in halves crosswise, cut off a thin slice from rounding part of each half. Sprinkle with salt and pepper, dip in crumbs, place in a well-buttered broiler and broil six to eight minutes.

STUFFED TOMATOES.

Take fine, large tomatoes, not too ripe. Cut out the blossom end and scoop out the inside as clean as you can without breaking the skins. Chop fine and add equal parts of ground chicken, green corn (uncooked), okra and a few bread crumbs. Season well with salt and pepper and a very little onion juice. Fill skins, put a piece of butter on top of each, and place in a baking dish (buttered) and bake in a good oven.

BRUSSELS SPROUTS IN WHITE SAUCE.

Pick over, remove wilted leaves and soak in cold water fifteen minutes. Cook in boiling salted water twenty minutes, or until easily pierced with a skewer. Drain, and to each pint add one cup white sauce.

BOILED CUCUMBERS.

Old cucumbers may be pared, cut in pieces, cooked until soft in boiling salted water, drained, mashed and seasoned with butter, salt and pepper.

FRIED CUCUMBERS.

Pare cucumbers and cut lengthwise in one-third inch slices. Dry between towels, sprinkle with salt and pepper, dip in crumbs, egg and crumbs again, fry in deep fat, and drain.

EGG PLANT A LA CREOLE.

Boil whole in salt water until done, but not over done. Cut in half and scoop out the meat, leaving enough in skin to form a shell. Mash the meat of egg plant, salt and pepper to taste, add the juice of a small onion, three fourths of a pint of toasted bread crumbs. Soften with a little milk, and add a can of dry shrimp chopped fine. Put back in shells with crumbs sprinkled on the top. Place a lump of butter the size of a walnut on each shell and slip in oven until a light brown.

STUFFED EGG PLANT.

Cook egg plant fifteen minutes in boiling salted water to cover. Cut a slice from top, and with a spoon remove pulp, taking care not to work too closely to skin. Chop pulp, and add one cup soft stale bread crumbs. Melt two tablespoons butter, add one-half tablespoon finely chopped onion, and cook five minutes; or try out three slices of bacon, using bacon fat in place of butter. Add to chopped pulp and bread, season with salt and pepper, and if necessary moisten with a little stock or water; cook five minutes, cool slightly, and add one beaten egg. Refill egg plant, cover with buttered bread crumbs, and bake twenty-five minutes in a hot oven.

BAKED BANANAS.

Peel firm bananas and cut lengthwise; place in a baking dish. Slice a lemon very thin, put a layer of banana with three slices of lemon, and then a layer of banana and three slices of lemon, sprinkled well with sugar. Put in the oven to bake.

CROQUETTES OF FRENCH PEAS.

2 tablespoonfuls of butter.	2 tablespoonsful of flour.
1 pint of cream.	Yolk of 1 egg.
2 cans of peas.	Salt, pepper and celery salt.
1 teaspoonful onion juice.	

Melt butter and flour together, then add the cream and seasonings and the well-beaten yolk of egg, and then the peas, which have been put through a puree strainer. Pour out on to a platter to cool, roll into croquettes, and fry as chicken croquettes.

BOILED RICE.

1 cup rice.	2 quarts boiling water.
1 tablespoon salt.	

Pick over rice; add slowly to boiling, salted water, so as not to check boiling of water. Boil thirty minutes, or until soft. Drain in coarse strainer, and pour over one quart hot water; return to kettle in which it was cooked; cover, place on back of range, and let stand to dry off, when kernels are distinct. When stirring rice, always use a fork to avoid breaking kernels. Rice is more satisfactory when soaked over night in cold water to cover.

SWEET POTATOES AU GRATIN.

Cut five medium-sized cold boiled sweet potatoes in one-third inch slices. Put a layer in buttered baking-dish, sprinkle with salt, pepper, and three tablespoons brown sugar, dot over with one tablespoon butter. Repeat, cover with buttered cracker crumbs, and bake until the crumbs are brown. Good with game or meat.

ENTREES

CHICKEN WITH ASPARAGUS TIPS.

2 cups very tender chicken breast. 1 tablespoonful of butter.
1 cup cooked asparagus tips   ½ pint cream.
   (fresh or canned.)   Yolks of 2 hard-boiled eggs.

Rub the yolks and butter to a paste and add the cream. Stir until thoroughly blended. Season with salt and pepper; then lay in the asparagus tips and chicken and cook for a few minutes. Delicious patty filling.

SUPREME OF CHICKEN.

Breast and wing of one large chicken (raw), four eggs, two-thirds of cup of thick cream; season with salt, pepper and celery salt. Force chicken through meat grinder. Beat eggs separately and add, stirring until mixture is smooth. Add cream and seasoning. Butter timbal molds or one large mold with stem in center. Serve with center filled with peas and on edge of peas and line with chopped mushrooms or truffles, then fill with the chicken, and set molds in a pan of boiling water and bake about thirty minutes. Serve with bechamel sauce.

CHICKEN CROQUETTES.

Boil one chicken and grind the meat with one can mushrooms; soak one-half pound stale bread in the broth nd add to meat and mushrooms; add one-quarter of a pound of butter and four eggs, mix all well together and boil until well cooked, season with salt, pepper, celery salt, chopped parsley, a little finely chopped onion and a very little grated nutmeg. Pour out on a platter; when thoroughly cold, shape, roll in bread crumbs and fry in boiling fat.

STUFFED CHICKEN LEGS.

Breast of one chicken.	1 cup of cream.
Whites of two eggs.	3 tablespoons butter
1 tablespoon onion.	3 table spoons flour.
1 tablespoon fresh mushrooms.	½ teaspoon salt.
1 small truffle.	Little pepper.

1 tablespoon sherry wine.

Melt butter, add chopped onion, mushrooms and truffle, broil a few minutes. Remove onions, mushrooms and truffle. Add flour, and when thoroughly blended add cream, salt and pepper, cook until thick; then add the sherry wine. Add the onions, mushrooms and truffle and the breast of a raw chicken, which has been ground and thoroughly mixed with the whites of two eggs; add to the other mixture. Spread out on a dish to cool. Remove bone from leg of the chicken (raw); fill with the mixture, sew up and broil in butter. Serve hot or cold. If served hot, serve with drawn butter. Delicious cold.

CHICKEN BREAST SMOTHERED IN MUSHROOMS.

Remove the breast from a chicken which has been partially boiled. Then remove the skin from the breast. Put in a pan with three tablespoons of butter, cover with fresh mushrooms and put in a hot oven. Cook until mushrooms are thoroughly done and breast is tender. Remove from the oven and add a little flour and cream to the butter in which chicken and mushrooms have been broiled; season with salt and pepper, and serve.

SWEETBREAD CROQUETTES.

2 pairs sweetbreads.   A few chopped mushrooms.
1 level tablespoonful of butter.   1 heaping tablespoon of flour,
1 cup of cream.   salt, pepper and a little onion
                                juice.

Parboil the sweetbreads, putting a little lemon juice in the water. Throw them into cold water. Remove the outside skin and membrane. Chop fine and measure. Add enough chopped mushrooms to make a pint. Melt the butter and add the flour and then the cream. When smooth, add the yelk of one egg. Season with salt, pepper and a little onion juice, chopped parsley and celery salt. Then add the sweetbreads and mushrooms. Cook a few minutes, turn out to cool, shape, dip in bread crumbs, diluted eggs and crumbs, place in a frying-basket and fry in hot lard.

SWEETBREAD A LA DIPLOMAT.

Saute one-half tablespoon of chopped onion in two tablespoons of butter. Add two tablespoons of flour, one cup of white stock and cream, season with salt and cayenne. Add yolk of one egg. When it thickens, add one third cup of mushrooms, chopped fine, two tablespoons of chopped truffles, trimmings of the sweetbreads, and a little chopped parsley. Then add one tablespoon of sherry wine. Let it cool and spread on sweetbreads which have been sauted in butter (after parboiling), dip in eggs, bread crumbs and eggs, and fry in hot fat. Serve with allemande sauce.

SWEETBREAD CUTLETS.

Boil two pairs of sweetbreads in salt water with a tablespoonful of lemon juice; drain and cover with cold water. When cold, chop fine and add sufficient chopped mushrooms to make one pint in all. Melt one tablespoonful of butter, add one tablespoonful of flour, salt and pepper to taste. When smooth add slowly a cup of cream. When this thickens, add a tablespoonful of lemon juice and a slight grating of nutmeg, half a teaspoon of finely chopped parsley, one beaten egg, and the sweetbreads and mushrooms. Pour out on a dish to cool; make palm shape, roll in bread crumbs, diluted egg and bread crumbs, place in frying basket and fry in hot lard. Serve with allemande sauce.

LITTLE PIGS IN BLANKETS.

Select large, plump oysters, or firm pieces of sweetbread which have been parboiled. Wrap them in thin slices of fat bacon, pinning with a wooden toothpick. Broil in a little butter.

STUFFED PEPPERS.

Cut off the tops of green peppers and remove the seed, parboil them ten minutes, chop the tops fine, one tablespoonful of chopped onion and two of fresh chopped mushrooms; saute all in two tablespoonfuls of butter about twelve minutes, add one tablespoon of flour, half a cup of brown stock, one tablespoon of ground chicken, one-half tablespoon of ground ham, and one tablespoon of bread crumbs. Season with salt, pepper and chopped parsley, cool, then stuff the peppers, sprinkle with buttered bread crumbs and put in the oven to brown; serve with white sauce.

STUFFED MUSHROOMS.

Cut off the caps, peel, scrape out and saute in butter. Then chop fine a little onion, and two tablespoons of chopped mushrooms, and saute in two tablespoons of butter. Add one heaping tablespoon of flour, one-third of a cup of brown stock, and one-quarter of a cup of cream. Season with salt, cayenne, and chopped parsley, and when thick, add a little ground chicken, ground ham, and sweetbreads. When cold, put through pastry bag on to mushrooms, cover with buttered bread crumbs, and put in oven to brown. Serve on round toast with mushroom sauce.

PEPPER TIMBALS.

Butter well a tin timbal mold or cup, line with a large red pepper from which have been taken the seeds (and which has been parboiled, or use the canned red pepper), butter them and line with chopped mushrooms. Drop into each one a raw egg, sprinkle over a little salt and pepper, put into a baking pan which is half full of boiling water, and put into a hot oven and cook until the egg is thoroughly done. Turn out and serve with white sauce.

MUSHROOMS A L'ALGONQUIN.

Wash, peel and remove the stems from large, selected mushrooms and then saute in butter; when done, put in a buttered pan, placing on each a large oyster; sprinkle with salt and pepper, place on each a bit of butter, cook in a hot oven until the oysters are plump. Serve with drawn butter sauce.

EGGS A LA TURK.

Brown one chicken liver and one large mushroom together in butter one minute. Add a little chopped onion, salt and pepper, and a tablespoonful of flour; beat until smooth. Then add one tablespoon of sherry and enough brown stock to make a sauce—about half a cupful—one teaspoonful of lemon juice, and a few chopped truffles. Place a poached egg, well cooked, on round buttered toast, and serve the sauce around it.

SWEETBREADS A LA NAPOLI.

Parboil a large sweetbread and cut in eight pieces. Cook in hot frying-pan with a small quantity of butter, adding enough beef extract to give sweetbread a glazed appearance. Cut bread in slices, shape with a circular cutter three and one-half inches in diameter, and toast. Spread each piece with two tablespoons grated Parmesan cheese seasoned with salt and paprika and moistened with two tablespoons heavy cream. Arrange one piece of sweetbread on each piece of toast and season with salt and pepper. Put in individual glass-covered dishes, having two tablespoons cream in each dish. Cover each piece of sweetbread with sauted mushroom cap, put on glass covers, and bake in a moderate oven eight minutes.

Miss Farmer.

CHESTNUT CROQUETTES.

1 cup mashed French chestnuts.	Yolks 2 eggs.
2 tablespoons thick cream.	1 teaspoon sugar.

¼ teaspoon vanilla.

Mix ingredients in order given. Shape in balls, dip in crumbs, egg, and crumbs again, fry in deep fat, and drain.

CROUSTADES OF BREAD.

Cut stale bread in two inch slices. Remove centers, leaving cases. Fry in deep fat or brush over with melted butter, and brown in oven. Fill with creamed vegetables, fish, or meat.

BAKED EGGS IN TOMATOES.

Eggs may be baked in small tomatoes. Cut a slice from stem end of tomato, scoop out the pulp, slip in an egg, sprinkle with salt and pepper, cover with buttered crumbs, and bake. Serve on toast.

SWEETBREAD CUTLETS WITH ASPARAGUS TIPS.

Parboil a sweetbread, split, and cut in pieces shaped like a small cutlet, or cut in circular pieces. Sprinkle with salt and pepper, dip in crumbs, egg, and crumbs, and saute in butter. Arrange in a circle around Creamed Asparagus Tips.

DEVILLED CRABS.

1 cup chopped crab meat.	Yolks 2 eggs.
¼ cup mushrooms, finely chopped.	2 tablespoons Sherry wine.
2 tablespoons butter.	1 teaspoon finely chopped parsley.
2 tablespoons flour.	Salt and pepper.
⅔ cup White Stock.	

Make a sauce of butter, flour, and stock; add yolks of eggs, seasonings (except parsley), crab meat, and mushrooms. Cook three minutes, add parsley, and cool mixture. Wash and trim crab shells, fill rounding with mixture, sprinkle with stale bread crumbs mixed with a small quantity of melted butter. Bake until crumbs are brown.

QUEEN FRITTERS.

¼ cup butter (scant).	½ cup flour.
½ cup boiling water.	2 eggs.
Fruit preserve or marmalade.	

Put butter in small saucepan and pour on water. As soon as water again reaches boiling-point, add flour all at once and stir until mixture leaves sides of saucepan, cleaving to spoon. Remove from fire and add eggs unbeaten, one at a time, beating mixture thoroughly between addition of eggs. Drop by spoonfuls and fry in deep fat until well puffed and browned. Drain, make an opening, and fill with preserve or marmalade.

SAUCES

ALLEMANDE SAUCE.

Melt two level tablespoonfuls of butter, and add two heaping tablespoonfuls of flour; when smooth, pour on one-half pint of white stock and one-half pint of cream; season with salt, pepper, chopped parsley and lemon juice, and then add the beaten yolk of an egg.

BECHAMEL SAUCE.

1½ cups white stock.	1 slice of onion.
1 slice of carrot.	1 bay leaf.
1 sprig of parsley.	¼ cup of butter.
¼ cup of flour.	1 cup of cream.
Salt and pepper.	

Cook the stock with the onion, carrot, bay leaf and parsley about fifteen minutes, and then strain. Melt the butter, add the flour, then the stock and cream.

WHITE SAUCE.

2 tablespoons butter.	1 cup milk.
2 tablespoons flour.	¼ teaspoon salt.
Few grains pepper.	

Put butter in saucepan, stir until melted and bubbling; add flour mixed with seasonings, and stir until thoroughly blended. Pour on gradually the milk, adding about one-third at a time, stirring until well mixed, then beating until smooth and glossy. If a wire whisk is used, all the milk may be added at once; and although more quickly made if milk is scalded, it is not necessary.

HOLLANDAISE SAUCE.

½ cup of butter.   ½ teaspoon of salt.
Yolks of 4 uncooked eggs.   ⅛ cup of boiling water.
1½ tablespoonfuls lemon juice. Dash of cayenne.

Fill a bowl with hot water, pour out the water and wipe
the bowl dry. Put the butter into it and beat until soft
and creamy; add the yolks of the eggs, one by one, and
beat until they are blended with the butter. Add the
lemon juice, salt and pepper, and beat again until smooth.
Then take out the spoon and beat the mixture with an
egg beater five minutes. Put into a double boiler with
boiling water. Add to the butter and eggs one-third cup
of boiling water and cook until the same is as thick as mayonnaise, beating constantly with the egg beater. Serve
either hot or cold.

MUSHROOM SAUCE.

Two tablespoons of butter, two and one-half tablespoons of flour, one cup of brown stock, one-half slice of
onion, one-quarter can of mushrooms, cut up. Cook onion
in butter until slightly browned, and remove onion. Add
flour and seasonings, and then add stock gradually, and
when perfectly smooth add mushrooms.

HORSERADISH SAUCE.

Mix two tablespoonfuls of grated horseradish with one
tablespoonful of vinegar and one-fourth teaspoonful each
of salt and pepper. Mix thoroughly and stir in four tablespoonfuls of whipped cream, stiff. Serve with roast beef
or oysters.

SAUCE FOR STUFFED PEPPERS OR FISH.

½ cup of butter.   ½ cup of cream.
1 teaspoon of flour.

Cook in a double boiler, stirring all the time. Cook until it becomes a thick sauce. When ready to serve, add salt and red pepper, one tablespoon of blanched almonds and about five chopped olives.

CUCUMBER SAUCE.

1 large cucumber.   ½ cup whipped cream.
4 drops of onion juice.   ½ teaspoon salt.
½ teaspoon of parsley.   Few grains pepper.
½ teaspoon Tarragon vinegar.

Chop fine one large cucumber, add salt and cayenne pepper to taste, add onion juice, parsley chopped fine, vinegar and whipped cream.

LOBSTER SAUCE.

2 tablespoonfuls of butter.   2 tablespoonfuls of flour.
1 pint of cream.   Yolks of 2 eggs.

Season with salt, pepper and a little sherry wine. Melt the butter, then add the flour, then the cream, then the seasoning, and then the well-beaten yolks, and when thick add a heaping cup of lobster, chopped fine.

MINT SAUCE.

¼ cup finely chopped mint leaves. 1 tablespoon powdered sugar.
½ cup vinegar.

Add sugar to vinegar; when dissolved, pour over mint and let stand thirty minutes on back of range to infuse. If vinegar is very strong dilute with water.

MAITRE D'HOTEL BUTTER.

¼ cup butter.	⅛ teaspoon pepper.
½ teaspoon salt.	½ tablespoon finely chopped
¾ tablespoon lemon juice.	parsley.

Put butter in a bowl, and with small wooden spoon work until creamy. Add salt, pepper and parsley, then lemon juice very slowly.

TOMATO SAUCE I (Without Stock).

½ can tomatoes, or	3 tablespoons butter.
1¾ cups fresh stewed tomatoes.	2½ tablespoons flour.
1 slice onion.	¼ teaspoon salt.
⅛ teaspoon pepper.	

Cook onion with tomatoes fifteen minutes, rub through a strainer, and add to butter and flour (to which seasonings have been added) cooked together. If tomatoes are very acid add a few grains of soda.

TOMATO SAUCE II.

½ can tomatoes.	½ teaspoon salt.
2 teaspoons sugar.	4 tablespoons butter.
8 peppercorns.	4 tablespoons flour.
Bit of bay leaf.	1 cup brown stock.

Cook tomatoes twenty minutes with sugar, peppercorns, bay leaf and salt; rub through a strainer and add stock. Brown the butter, add flour, and when well browned, gradually add hot liquid.

TOMATO CREAM SAUCE.

½ can tomatoes.	Bit of bay leaf.
Sprig of thyme.	1 cup White Sauce I.
1 stalk celery.	½ teaspoon salt.
1 slice onion.	Few grains cayenne.

¼ teaspoon soda.

Cook tomatoes twenty minutes with seasonings; rub through a strainer, add soda, then White Sauce. Serve with Baked Fish.

SALADS

CUCUMBER, CELERY AND SWEETBREAD SALAD.

Equal proportions of cucumber, celery and sweetbreads, which have been parboiled. Cut into small pieces and serve with mayonnaise or French dressing. Garnish with water cress or serve in head lettuce.

CUCUMBER AND CELERY SALAD.

Equal proportions of cucumber and celery. Cut cucumber and celery into small pieces and serve with mayonnaise dressing.

FROZEN TOMATO SALAD.

Take one quart can of tomatoes (or the same proportion of fresh tomatoes), drain off all the liquor, pour over them mayonnaise and a little chopped celery, put in a freezer and freeze. Serve in nasturtium leaves.

CHICKEN SALAD.

Take equal proportions of cold chicken and celery, cut not too small. To a quart of chicken and celery pour over one-half cup of French dressing and let it marinate half or whole morning, and when ready to serve mix with mayonnaise dressing.

NUT AND CELERY SALAD.

Mix equal parts of pecans, almonds, English walnuts, and celery. Marinate in oil, and serve with a French dressing with a border of curly celery.

TOMATOES STUFFED WITH CHEESE.

Take equal proportions of Neufchatel and Roquefort cheese and blend well together; mix with mayonnaise dressing. Remove centers out of tomatoes, fill with the cheese and serve on lettuce leaf.

PINEAPPLE AND NUT SALAD.

1 can pineapple.   1 cup English walnuts.

Remove the juice from the pineapple, cut into pieces about the size of an English walnut; add the walnuts and serve with whipped cream or mayonnaise.

WALDORF SALAD.

Mix equal quantities of finely cut apple and celery, and moisten with mayonnaise dressing. Garnish with curled celery and canned pimentoes cut in strips or fancy shapes. An attractive way of serving this salad is to remove tops from red or green apples, scoop out inside pulp, leaving just enough adhering to skin to keep apples in shape. Refill shells thus made with the salad, replace tops and serve on lettuce leaves.

LOBSTER SALAD.

1 cup of boiled lobster.   ½ cup chopped celery.

Mix together and serve with mayonnaise dressing. Serve in lobster shell, red apples or lettuce leaf.

WATER CRESS SALAD.

Freshen the water cress in very cold water until it becomes crisp. Dry thoroughly without bruising. Mix with it two sour apples sliced thin and French dressing.

ALBERTINE SALAD.

Arrange bunches of lettuce and watercress lengthwise of salad dish. Through center of dish put slices of fresh pear overlapping each other, and pour over Alberta Mayonnaise.

ALBERTA MAYONNAISE.

Dilute ½ cup mayonnaise with heavy cream to make of right consistency to pour easily. Add 3 tablespoons finely cut English walnut meats and season with salt and lemon juice.

CUPID'S DECEITS.

Salt halves of English walnut meats. Make balls of cream cheese, mashed and seasoned with salt and paprika then mixed with stoned chopped olives; flatten and place halves of nuts opposite each other on each piece. Roll each in wheat crispies pounded and sifted. Mould in aspen. Serve with salad.

PEPPER AND GRAPE FRUIT SALAD.

Cut slices from stem ends of six green peppers, and remove seeds. Refill with grape fruit pulp, finely cut celery and English walnut meats broken in pieces, allowing twice as much grape fruit as celery, and two nut meats to each pepper. Arrange on chicory or lettuce leaves and serve.

SWISS SALAD.

Mix one cup cold cooked chicken, cut in cubes, one cucumber pared and cut in cubes, one cup chopped English walnut meats, and one cup French peas. Marinate with French dressing, arrange on serving dish and garnish with mayonnaise dressing.

GREEN GRAPE SALAD.

Select firm, acid grapes; serve in a head of lettuce with
the cooked mayonnaise, only with a little more cream
added to it, or with a cream dressing, for which mix half a
teaspoonful of salt, half a teaspoonful of mustard, one-
fourth teaspoonful of sugar, one egg beaten slightly, two
tablespoonfuls of oil, three-fourths cup of rich cream and
a scant quarter of a cup of vinegar.

TOMATO JELLY.

Cook one-half can of tomatoes for ten minutes, with a
pinch of soda if very acid.   Add half a teaspoonful of salt
and rub through a sieve or strainer.   Pour over it one-
fourth box of gelatine which has been soaked in one-fourth
cup of cold water; mold, and when congealed, serve on
lettuce with mayonnaise dressing.

SALAD A LA JARDINE.

To one pint of ground, boiled chicken, add equal parts
of asparagus tips, peas, chopped string beans, chopped celery and a few pecan kernels.   Mix carefully and pour
over it mayonnaise.

EGG SALAD.

Boil the eggs twenty minutes.   Peel off the shells and
cut the eggs in half lengthwise.   Remove the yolks, put
in a bowl and cream.   Take two eggs well beaten, half a
teaspoonful of dry mustard, three tablespoonfuls of rich,
sweet cream, one tablespoonful of salt, one teaspoonful of
pepper, two tablespoonfuls of olive oil, and one and a half
tablespoonfuls of vinegar.   Boil all until very thick and
mix with the cooked yolks.   Fill the whites, and when
cold serve with mayonnaise.

MOQUIN SALAD.

Drain slices of canned pineapple and cut in halves crosswise. Arrange on lettuce leaves. Work one-half cream cheese with a wooden spoon, and moisten with French dressing. Force through a potato ricer over pineapple. Serve with French dressing.

FRENCH FRUIT SALAD.

2 oranges.	12 English walnut meats.
3 bananas	1 head lettuce.
½ lb. Malaga grapes.	French Dressing.

Peel oranges, and remove pulp separately from each section. Peel bananas, and cut in one-fourth inch slices. Remove skins and seeds from grapes. Break walnut meats in pieces. Mix prepared ingredients and arrange on lettuce leaves. Serve with French Dressing or Whipped Cream Mayonnaise.

HUNGARIAN SALAD.

Mix equal parts shredded fresh pineapple, bananas cut in pieces, and sections of tangerines, and marinate with French dressing. Fill banana skins with mixture, sprinkle generously with paprika, and arrange on lettuce leaves. Serve with Whipped Cream Mayonnaise.

ASPARAGUS SALAD.

Drain and rinse stalks of canned asparagus. Cut rings from a bright red pepper one-third inch wide. Place three or four stalks in each ring. Arrange on lettuce leaves and serve with French Dressing, to which has been added one-half tablespoon tomato catsup.

BERKSHIRE SALAD.

Marinate one cup cold boiled fowl cut into dice and one cup cooked French chestnuts broken in pieces with French Dressing. Add one finely chopped red pepper from which seeds have been removed, one cup celery cut into small pieces, and Mayonnaise.

PARISIAN FRENCH DRESSING.

½ cup olive oil.	2 tablespoons finely chopped parsley.
5 tablespoons vinegar.	
½ teaspoon powdered sugar.	4 red peppers.
1 tablespoon finely chopped.	8 green peppers.
Bermuda onion.	1 teaspoon salt.

Mix ingredients in the order given. Let stand one hour, then stir vigorously for five minutes. This is especially fine with lettuce, romaine, chicory, or endive. The red and green peppers are the small ones found in pepper sauce.

SALAD DRESSING

MAYONNAISE No. 1.

Yolk of 1 hard-boiled egg.	1 teaspoonful of mustard.
Salt and pepper to taste.	Yolk of 1 raw egg, well beaten.
½ of small bottle olive oil.	Vinegar to taste.

White of 1 egg beaten stiff and dry.

Rub the yolk of hard boiled egg through a fine sieve until smooth; add to that the mustard, salt, pepper, raw yolk, well beaten. Then add the oil, and next the vinegar slowly, lastly the raw white of egg.

WALTHAM SALAD DRESSING.

Mix two teaspoons each salt and sugar, one teaspoon mustard and one-eighth teaspoon pepper. Add one egg slightly beaten, one-quarter cup vinegar and one cup sour cream. Cook in double boiler until mixture thickens.

MAYONNAISE No. 2 (Cooked).

Yolks of two eggs, well beaten, four tablespoonfuls of vinegar. Boil until thick, and stir in one heaping tablespoonful of butter or olive oil. When cold, add half a teaspoonful of salt, half a teaspoonful of dry mustard and a little pepper, and a cup of whipped cream.

POTATO MAYONNAISE DRESSING.

1 small baked potato.	1 teaspoon powdered sugar.
1 teaspoon mustard.	2 tablespoonfuls vinegar.
1 teaspoon salt.	¾ cup olive oil or Snowflake oil.

Smooth and mash the inside of a potato, add mustard, salt and powdered sugar; add one tablespoon of vinegar, and rub mixture through a fine sieve. Add oil and remaining vinegar. One would hardly realize eggs were not used in the mixture.

RUSSIAN DRESSING.

To three-fourths cup mayonnaise dressing, add three tablespoons chili sauce, two tablespoons pimentos cut in small pieces, one tablespoon tarragon vinegar, one teaspoon chives cut in tiny pieces, three fourths teaspoon Escoffier Sauce, and enough dried and finely pounded tarragon leaves to flavor. Serve with lettuce.

BRETTON WOODS SALAD.

Fill orange baskets with sections of orange and small pieces of apple, using twice as much orange as apple. Marinate with Fruit French Dressing and garnish each with one section of apple between two sections of orange. Arrange on lettuce leaves for individual service.

DRESSING FOR COLD SLAW.

6 yolks of eggs.	2 tablespoons of fine sugar.
Tablespoon butter.	1 cup of vinegar.
Teaspoon of made mustard.	½ teaspoon of salt.

Beat the eggs well. Cook in a double boiler with vinegar, sugar, butter, salt and mustard, beating all the time. When nearly done, add the juice of one lemon. When thick remove from the fire and when cold whip in one-half cupful of cream. Mix well, and put in a cold place until ready to serve.

ASTORIA DRESSING.

To one-half cup mayonnaise, add slowly one-half cup French dressing. When well mixed add one-fourth cup tomato catsup, one tablespoon chopped green peppers, one teaspoon powdered sugar and six drops of Tabasco Sauce.

GERMAN DRESSING.

Beat one-half cup of heavy cream, just beginning to sour, with one egg; beat until stiff. Add three tablespoonfuls of vinegar and beat again. Fine for fruit salads.

FRENCH DRESSING.

½ teaspoon salt.	2 tablespoons of vinegar.
¼ teaspoon pepper.	4 tablespoons of oil.

Mix ingredients and stir until well blended.

Note—2 drops of creme de menthe added to French dressing makes a delicious dressing; and very crisp bacon added to French dressing makes a delicious dressing for lettuce.

SALAD CREAM.

Mix one-half tablespoonful of mustard and salt (each) and one tablespoonful of sugar with one egg, slightly beaten. Pour on this three-fourths cup of cream and one-fourth cup of scalded vinegar with two and a half tablespoonfuls melted butter. Cook in a double boiler until it thickens slightly. Strain and cool. Serve on cold slaw.

FRUIT FRENCH DRESSING.

Mix one-half teaspoon salt, one-fourth teaspoon pepper one-eighth teaspoon paprika, one-fourth cup each orange juice and olive oil, two tablespoons lemon juice and one teaspoon powdered sugar. Shake well before serving.

SANDWICHES

In preparing sandwiches cut the slices of bread as thin as possible and remove the crusts. If butter is used, cream the butter and spread the bread before cutting from the loaf.

LETTUCE SANDWICH.

Spread bread with mayonnaise dressing and then place sliced lettuce between the slices.

CHICKEN SALAD SANDWICH.

Cut up equal proportions of chicken and celery fine. Mix with mayonnaise dressing and spread between plain bread.

PLAIN GROUND CHICKEN.

Grind chicken fine, moisten thoroughly with cream, season with salt, pepper and celery salt and spread between buttered bread.

NUT SANDWICHES.

Spread bread with mayonnaise dressing, and put chopped pecans between the slices.

CUCUMBER SANDWICHES.

Chop the cucumber, mix with tartar sauce and spread between bread.

RUSSIAN SANDWICH.

Spread Graham bread with mayonnaise dressing. Take equal parts of Neufchatel cheese and chopped olives and mix well together and spread between slices of bread.

PEANUT SANDWICH.

Spread bread (white or Graham bread) with French mustard. Pound roasted peanuts to a paste and spread between the slices.

CHEESE AND NUT.

Spread bread with mayonnaise dressing; mix Neufchatel cheese and nuts well together and spread between bread.

FIG SANDWICH.

Chop one dozen figs very fine, add hot water to moisten to a paste, cook in a double boiler two hours, flavor to taste with lemon. Put between thin slices of bread. Sprinkle with chopped nuts.

CLUB SANDWICH.

Spread toasted white bread with mayonnaise dressing, then a lettuce leaf, a slice of crisp bacon and a small slice of cold chicken between the slices of toast.

TOMATO SANDWICH.

Spread thin slices of bread with mayonnaise dressing seasoned with a few drops of onion juice. Place a slice of peeled tomato between them.

GARDEN SANDWICH.

Chop cucumbers, tomatoes, a little mild onion and capers. Mix together. Spread bread with mayonnaise and then the chopped vegetables, and lay on the other slice.

CHEESE BALLS.

1½ cups grated mild cheese   Few grains cayenne.
1 tablespoon flour.   Whites 3 eggs.
¼ teaspoon salt.   Cracker dust.

Mix cheese with flour and seasonings. Beat whites of eggs until stiff, and add to first mixture. Shape in small balls, roll in cracker dust, fry in deep fat, and drain on brown paper. Serve with salad course.

FRUIT SANDWICHES.

Remove stems and finely chop figs; add a small quantity of water, cook in double boiler until a paste is formed, then add a few drops of lemon juice. Cool mixture, and spread on thin slices of buttered bread; sprinkle with finely chopped nuts and cover with pieces of buttered bread.

EGG SANDWICHES.

Chop finely the white of "hard-boiled" eggs; force the yolks through a strainer or potato ricer. Mix yolks and whites, season with salt and pepper, and moisten with Mayonnaise or Cream Salad Dressing. Spread mixture between thin slices of buttered bread.

CHEESE AND BACON SANDWICHES.

Rub into one cake of Neufchatel Cheese the yolk of one raw egg, one tablespoonful of sweet cream, one of Worcestershire and paprika and salt to taste. Fold in the white of egg beaten stiff, spread on thin slice of bread, on top of each slice place a thin slice of bacon, set in oven until baked crisp, serve hot. This will make six sandwiches.

DESSERTS

PLAIN PASTRY.

1½ cups flour.	¼ cup of butter.
¼ cup lard.	½ teaspoonful salt.

A little ice water.

Wash the butter, squeeze out all the milk and water, flatten it out. Add the salt to the flour and cut in the lard with a knife. Moisten it with the cold water. Toss on the board, dredged sparingly with flour, pat and roll out. Fold in the butter, roll out, and repeat folding and rolling several times. Cover with cheesecloth and set away in a cool place, though never in direct contact with ice. Roll thin and bake in a moderate oven.

FILLING FOR LEMON PIE.

2 lemons.	3 tablespoons flour.
2 cups of sugar.	1 tablespoon butter.
2 cups of hot water.	4 eggs.

Whites for top of pies. Boil until thick, bake crust and fill. Filling makes two pies.

COCOANUT FILLING.

One half of a cup of butter, two cups of sugar, mixed well. Add the yolks of five eggs well beaten, one cup of milk, one tablespoon of flour, and one cup of grated cocoanut. Flavor with vanilla and cook until thick. W h e n cold, fill (cooked) pie crust and cover with meringue and put in the oven to brown.

BUTTERMILK PIES.

1 pint of buttermilk.	1 teaspoon cream of tartar.
2 teacups of sugar.	3 tablespoons of flour.
1 tablespoon butter.	5 to 7 eggs.

Use whites for the meringue. Boil this to a custard and fill the pie crusts and bake.

MERINGUE.

Add sugar enough to whites to make thick and stiff; spread over pies and put in oven to brown a few minutes.

SUGAR PIES.

Four eggs beaten separately, one pint of brown sugar, one tablespoon of butter, one cup of cream. Boil all together and when thick fill the pastry and bake.

JELLY PIES.

4 eggs beaten separately.	1 glass of jelly (plum jelly best).
1½ cups of sugar.	1 tablespoon of flour.
	1 tablespoon of butter.

Mix the butter and sugar together, then flour, then the jelly, then the eggs. Beat well and fill pastry and bake.

ENGLISH PLUM PUDDING.

½ pound stale bread crumbs.	½ cup wine and brandy mixed.
¼ pound sugar.	1 cup hot milk.
½ nutmeg, grated.	1 teaspoonful cinnamon.
½ teaspoonful mace and ground cloves.	4 eggs.
	½ pound beef suet.
1 teaspoonful salt.	¼ pound currants.
1½ pounds raisins.	⅛ pound citron.
¼ pound figs.	

Soak the stale bread crumbs in one cup of hot milk. When cold, add the sugar and yolks of eggs beaten stiff, also nutmeg, cinnamon, mace, ground cloves and salt. Chop fine and cream the beef suet and add to the mixture with the raisins stoned and floured, and the currants, figs and citron chopped fine. Add the wine and brandy, and the whites of four eggs beaten stiff. Turn into a buttered mold and steam from six to eight hours.

Boston Cooking School.

CHEESE CAKES.

Melt two tablespoons butter, three and one-half tablespoons flour and four tablespoons grated American cheese. Fold into the whites of three eggs beaten stiff. Season with one-fourth teaspoon salt and a few grains cayenne. Drop from tip of spoon to a buttered sheet one inch apart, and bake in a moderate oven from ten to fifteen minutes. Serve with salad.

PEACH CONSERVE.

Soak one pound dried, skinned peaches in one quart cold water over night, add one cup raisins cut in pieces, one-half pound English walnut meats cut in pieces, juice of one lemon, juice of one orange, one orange thinly sliced and one pound sugar. Let simmer one and one-quarter hours. Serve in patties.

MACAROON PUDDING.

½ dozen eggs.	1 glass sherry.
2 dozen macaroons.	½ cup of cream.
	½ cup sugar.

Beat yolks and sugar together, put in the cream, then the sherry. Put in double boiler and cook to a custard. Line a baking or pudding dish with the macaroons, and pour the custard over them. Whip the whites of eggs to a stiff froth and pour over the custard.   Stick in blanched almonds quite thick and brown in the oven.   Serve hot or cold.

BREAD PUDDING.

Crumble one loaf of bread and pour on it one and one-half pints of boiling milk.   Beat six eggs; add to bread also one tea cup of sugar, a piece of butter, size of an egg half pound of raisins sprinkled with a little flour, one wine glass of wine or brandy, one-half teaspoonful of ground cinnamon.   Stir all together and bake.   Serve with hard sauce.

BROWN BETTY.

Butter a deep pudding dish.   Place a layer of finely chopped apples in the bottom and add a layer of fine bread crumbs.   Sprinkle with sugar and a little spice; add a little butter, then another layer of apples and so on until your dish is full.   The top layer should be of crumbs, sugar and spice.   Bake in a moderate oven until quite brown.   Serve with either cream or hard sauce.

KISS PUDDING.

One-half pound of stale sponge cakes.   Put half of the cake in a pudding pan, then a layer of peaches, (canned ones are the best) then a layer of the cakes and last a layer of peaches.

Make a custard of one pint of milk, the yolks of three eggs; when thick pour over cake and peaches and put pudding in the oven for ten minutes.   Before serving pour whipped cream over top and decorate with candied cherries.

BISQUE PIE.

1 pint sweet milk.	6 macaroons.
6 tablespoons powdered sugar.	2 tablespoons of (chopped) candied
1½ tablespoons corn starch.	cherries.
Yolks of 6 eggs.	2 tablespoons of sultana raisins.
2 tablespoons of whisky or sherry.	

Boil the milk, sugar, corn starch and egg, in a double boiler, to a thick custard, then add macaroons (browned and crushed), fruit and liquor and mix thoroughly and fill two medium size pie crusts, baked and cold.

MERINGUE

Beat the six whites to a stiff froth with twelve ounces of sugar. Add three macaroons (browned and crushed) and one tablespoon of whiskey. Cover over the pies and brown slightly in a slow oven.

HAZELNUT CREAM PIE.

1 quart milk.	Yolks of 6 eggs.
6 tablespoons of sugar.	4 tablespoons of blanched hazelnuts.
1½ tablespoons corn starch.	½ teaspoon vanilla.

Boil milk, sugar, corn starch and eggs to a thick custard and add crushed, roasted nuts and vanilla. This will fill two crusts—cover with

MERINGUE

Beat the whites of six eggs to a stiff froth. Add twelve ounces powdered sugar. Spread over pies and sprinkle the top with crushed hazelnuts and powdered sugar. Put in oven and brown slightly.

RHUBARB PIE.

One and one-half cups (or a little more) rhubarb cut fine, one cup sugar, one tablespoonful flour, one tablespoonful butter, one egg well beaten, juice and grated rind of half a lemon. Mix all ingredients together, add rhubarb. This makes one pie (two crusts).

STUFFED FIGS.

Take a basket of pulled figs and soak over night in equal parts of sherry wine and water. Next morning sweeten liquor in which figs have been soaked, with half a teacup of sugar. Boil figs in this mixture for about ten minutes. Remove figs and boil syrup down. Take out the inside of figs and mix with a cup of chopped pecans, and a little sherry or brandy, and stuff the figs with the mixture. Pile on a platter, cover with remainder of the liquor. When cold put whipped cream around dish and serve.

MINCEMEAT PATTIES.

Heat patty shells and mincemeat separately. When very hot, fill the shells with the mincemeat and serve with frozen whipped cream, flavored with brandy.

FIG PUDDING.

⅓ pound beef suet.	1 teaspoonful salt.
2 heaping cups stale bread crumbs.	½ pound figs.
	1 cup sugar.
½ cup milk.	2 eggs well beaten.

Chop and rub to a cream the beef suet, add the figs finely chopped; mix thoroughly. To the bread crumbs add the well-beaten eggs, milk, sugar and salt, and mix all to-

gether well. Place in a buttered pudding dish and steam
for several hours. Serve with a fancy sauce.

SAUCE FOR SAME

Beat the yolks of two eggs until light. Then beat the
whites of two eggs stiff and add half a cup of powdered
sugar. Combine the two and add one-fourth cup of hot
cream and four tablespoonfuls sherry wine.

—*Boston Cooking School.*

CABINET PUDDING.

1 pint of milk.	½ cup raisins, chopped citron,
2 tablespoonfuls of sugar.	currants.
½ tablespoonful of butter.	¼ teaspoonful of salt.
2 eggs.	1½ pints stale sponge cake.

Beat the eggs, sugar and salt together; add the milk;
sprinkle a pudding mold with cake crumbs, then a layer of
fruit, then cake crumbs, and continue until all is used up.
Pour on the custard and let it stand two hours, then steam
one and a half hours.

SAUCE FOR SAME.

1 cup of butter.	½ cup of cream.	2 cups powdered sugar.

Beat the butter to a cream, add the sugar gradually,
and when very light, add the cream. Flavor to taste.
Cook for a few minutes in a double boiler.

RICE PUDDING.

4 tablespoonfuls of rice.	Milk and cream.
½ teaspoonful of salt.	4 tablespoonfuls sugar.
1 teaspoonful vanilla.	½ cup of stoned raisins.

Into a pudding-dish holding a quart put the rice, which
has been well washed and soaked. Fill the dish with milk
and cream, and add the salt. Put into the oven to cook

for about half an hour. Add the sugar, vanilla, and raisins, and return to the oven and cook slowly for two hours or more if necessary. If the milk boils down, lift the skin at the side and add a little more hot cream. To make the pudding creamy, it must be cooked very slowly and plenty of cream used. Just before serving, spread thickly over the top fresh marshmallows. Put in the oven just long enough for the marshmallows to swell. Before sending to the table, garnish with candied cherries or red jelly. Serve with whipped or plain cream.

PINEAPPLE PUDDING.

2¾ cups of scalded cream.	¼ cup of cold milk.
⅓ cup of corn starch.	¼ cup of sugar.
¼ teaspoonful of salt.	½ can grated pineapple.

Whites of three eggs, beaten stiff.

Mix the corn starch, sugar, salt and cold milk well, and add to the scalded cream in a double boiler, stirring constantly until it thickens. Cook from ten to fifteen minutes, add the eggs, then pineapple. Mold, congeal, and serve with whipped cream.

BAVARIAN CREAM.

⅓ box of gelatine.	½ cup of boiling water.
Sweeten and flavor to taste.	1 quart of whipped cream.

Soak the gelatine in the boiling water, sweeten and flavor to taste; add one quart of stiff whipped cream; put in molds and set away to congeal, and serve with whipped cream.

CHARLOTTE RUSSE.

White of 1 egg.	Sponge lady fingers.
⅓ box gelatine dissolved in ½	1 cup powdered sugar.
pint boiling water.	2 teaspoonfuls vanilla.
Yolks of 3 eggs.	Whip from 1 quart of cream.

Beat the white of an egg slightly, put a thin coating around a glass bowl, and then line with sponge lady fingers. Dissolve the gelatine in boiling water. When thoroughly dissolved, stir in the sugar, add the vanilla and the beaten yolks of three eggs; stir in the whip from a quart of cream, and when it stiffens some, pour into the bowl, lined with sponge cakes and garnish the top prettily with whipped cream.

CHOCOLATE PUDDING.

¼ cup butter.
1 cup sugar.
Yolks 2 eggs.
½ cup milk.
1 ⅜ cups flour.

3 teaspoons baking powder.
Whites 2 eggs.
1 ⅓ squares Baker's chocolate.
⅛ teaspoon salt.
¼ teaspoon vanilla.

Cream the butter, and add one-half the sugar gradually. Beat yolks of eggs until thick and lemon colored, and add, gradually, remaining sugar. Combine mixtures, and add milk alternately with flour mixed and sifted with baking powder and salt; then add whites of eggs beaten until stiff, melted chocolate, and vanilla. Bake in an angel-cake pan, remove from pan, cool, fill the center with whipped cream, sweetened and flavored, and pour around.

CHOCOLATE SAUCE.

Boil one cup sugar, one-half cup water, and a few grains cream-of-tartar until of the consistency of a thin syrup. Melt one and one-half squares Baker's chocolate and pour on gradually the hot syrup. Cool slightly, and flavor with one-fourth teaspoon vanilla.

SCALLOPED APPLES.

1 small baker's stale loaf.
¼ cup butter.
1 quart sliced apples.

¼ cup sugar.
¼ teaspoon grated nutmeg.
Grated rind and juice of ½ lemon.

Cut loaf in halves, remove soft part, and crumb by rubbing through a colander; melt butter and stir in lightly with fork; cover bottom of buttered pudding-dish with crumbs and spread over one-half the apples, sprinkle with one-half sugar, nutmeg, lemon juice, and rind mixed together; repeat cover with remaining crumbs, and bake forty minutes in moderate oven. Cover at first to prevent crumbs browning too rapidly. Serve with sugar and cream.

POOR MAN'S PUDDING.

4 cups milk.	½ teaspoon salt.
½ cup rice.	½ teaspoon cinnamon.
⅓ cup molasses.	1 tablespoon butter.

Wash rice, mix and bake same as Rice Pudding. At last stirring, add butter.

MOCK MINCE PIE.

4 common crackers, rolled.	1 cup raisins, seeded and chopped.
1½ cups sugar.	½ cup butter.
1 cup of molasses.	2 eggs well beaten.
⅓ cup lemon juice or vinegar.	Spices.

Mix ingredients in order given, adding spices to taste. Bake between crusts. This quantity will make two pies.

BANANA CANTELOUPE.

½ box gelatin or	⅔ cup sugar.
2 tablespoons granulated gelatine.	4 bananas, mashed pulp.
½ cup cold water.	1 tablespoon lemon juice.
Whites 2 eggs.	Whip from 3½ cups cream.
¼ cup powdered sugar.	12 lady fingers.
¾ cup scalded cream.	

Soak gelatine in cold water, beat whites of eggs slightly, add powdered sugar, and gradually hot cream, cook over hot water until it thickens; add soaked gelatine and re

maining sugar, strain into a pan set in ice-water, add bananas and lemon juice, stir until it begins to thicken, then
fold in whip from cream. Line a melon mould with lady
fingers trimmed to just fit sections of mould, turn in the
mixture, spread evenly, and chill. Garnish with whipped
cream.

ORANGE CHARLOTTE.

⅓ box gelatine or
1¼ tablespoons granulated
    gelatine.
⅓ cup cold water.
⅓ cup boiling water.

1 cup sugar.
3 tablespoons lemon juice.
1 cup orange juice and pulp.
Whites 3 eggs.
Whip from 2 cups cream.

Soak gelatine in cold water, dissolve in boiling water,
strain, and add sugar, lemon juice, orange juice, and pulp.
Chill in pan of ice-water; when quite thick, beat with wire
spoon or whisk until frothy, then add whites of eggs beaten
stiff, and fold in cream. Line a mould with sections of
oranges, turn in mixture, smooth evenly, and chill.

ANGEL CHARLOTTE.

Soak one-fourth cup maraschino cherries to cover one
hour; then cut in pieces. Cut one-half cup English walnut
meats in pieces and one-half pound marshmallow cut in
pieces. Beat one cup heavy cream until stiff, add two
tablespoons powdered sugar, one-half teaspoon vanilla and
three-fourths tablespoon gelatine dissolved in three tablespoons boiling water. When mixture begins to thicken,
add fruit, marshmallow and nut meats. Serve in an angel
cake from which the center has been removed, leaving thin
wall, cover with whipped cream.

BAKED CARAMEL CUSTARD WITH SAUCE.

Set a small saucepan, containing one-half cup of sugar, over the fire and stir the sugar gently. As the sugar loses water by evaporation it assumes the appearance of flake tapioca, and as the cooking continues it changes color, becoming caramel. Care must be taken that the caramel does not burn or become too dark in color. Scald four cups of milk, and add the caramel to the milk very carefully, and as soon as the two are well blended, pour the mixture on to five eggs slightly beaten; then add one half teaspoonful of salt and one teaspoonful of vanilla. Strain at once into a buttered melon mold, set the mold in a pan of hot water and bake in a slow oven until the custard is firm. Serve with caramel sauce.

SAUCE FOR SAME.

Put one-half cup of sugar into a saucepan over the fire and stir the sugar until it melts and becomes a light brown color. Add half a cup of boiling water, and allow the liquid to simmer ten minutes.

STRAWBERRY SPONGE.

Soak one-third box of gelatine in one-third cup of cold water; dissolve in one-third cup of boiling water; add one cup of sugar, juice of one lemon, and one cup of strawberry juice. Set vessel in a pan of ice water and stir until it thickens. Add the whites of three eggs beaten stiff; and whip from one pint of cream. Chill before serving. The cream may be omitted. If preserved strawberries are used less sugar is required.

COMPOTE OF FIGS.

One pint of figs scalded and soaked over night in brandy. Pile up on a platter and serve with whipped cream or serve with brandy.

BANBURY TARTS.

1 cup raisins.	1 egg.
1 cup sugar.	1 cracker.

Juice and grated rind 1 lemon.

Stone and chop raisins, add sugar, egg slightly beaten, cracker finely rolled and lemon juice and rind. Roll pastry one-eighth inch thick, and cut pieces three and one-half inches long by three inches wide. Put two teaspoons of mixture on each piece. Moisten edge with cold water half way round, fold over, press edges together with three-tined fork, first dipped in flour. Bake twenty minutes in slow oven.

SIMPLE DESSERT.

Lady fingers.	Bananas, sliced thin.
½ cup of sherry wine.	2 heaping tablespoonfuls of sugar.

Whipped cream.

Line a bowl with lady fingers, fill it half full of bananas sliced thin, pour over them about half a cup of sherry wine and a heaping tablespoonful of sugar, then fill the bowl with whipped cream.

PRESERVES IN HALF ORANGES.

Take half of an orange, scoop out all of the pulp, cut the edge in points, fill in with preserves—pineapple being prettiest—and serve with whipped cream.

CAKES

*FRUIT CAKE.

1 pound butter.	2 pounds raisins.
1 pound sugar.	1 pound currants.
1 pound flour.	½ pound figs.
½ pound citron.	½ pound pineapple.
½ pound candied cherries.	2 pounds almonds.
12 eggs.	1 tablespoon cinnamon.
2 nutmegs.	1 tablespoon allspice.
½ glass of wine.	1 cup of molasses.
½ glass of brandy.	2 teaspoons baking powder.

Cream the butter and sugar together. Add New Or-leans molasses, then eggs, which have been beaten sepa-rately, next the flour, which has been browned; then dis-solve two teaspoons of baking powder in a cup of cream or new milk, and add to the mixture. Then add the spices which have been dissolved in the tumblerful of liquor. Chop fruit and nuts, dredge with flour, and put in the bat-ter last. Bake slowly four hours.

PECAN CAKE.

1 pound sugar.	1 pound flour.
1 pound of butter.	10 eggs.
½ tumbler of brandy.	2 grated nutmegs.
1 pound raisins.	¼ pound of citron.

1½ pounds of pecan kernels.

Cream the butter and sugar until light. Add the eggs beaten separately, then the nutmeg stirred in the brandy,

---

*NOTE—This is the recipe which gave me my start in business.

then the flour, raisins, citron and pecan kernels. Pour
into buttered mold and bake half an hour longer than you
would a black cake, same size.

OATMEAL COOKIES.

2 cups of sugar.	2 teaspoonfuls soda.
1 cup of butter or lard.	3 eggs.
2 heaping cups of oatmeal.	2 teaspoonfuls of cinnamon.
4 cups of flour.	1 cup of chopped nuts.

1 cup of raisins.

Mix butter and sugar, add oatmeal, then the eggs
beaten, then the cinnamon, nuts and raisins and the flour.
Mix the soda with a little hot water and add to the mixture. Toss on a well floured board, roll out and cut. Line
a pan with buttered paper and bake in a moderately quick
oven. These are delicious.

VALENTINE COOKIES.

Cream one-fourth cup butter and lard mixed, add three-
fourths cup sugar, one egg well beaten, two tablespoons
milk, one-half teaspoon salt, one and one-half teaspoons
baking powder, one and one-half teaspoons vanilla, one-
half cup nut meats finely chopped and about one and one-
half cups flour. Roll, shape, bake and decorate.

GINGER COOKIES.

One pint molasses, one cup of lard boiled together a
minute or two. Add one even teaspoon of soda, stirred
in when mixture is cold; one tablespoonful of ginger or
enough to make them hot. Flour enough to roll. Bake
in a hot oven.

IMPERIAL CAKE.

1 pound butter.	1 pound light brown sugar.
1 pound flour.	2 pounds raisins.
10 eggs.	2 pounds blanched almonds.
6 grated nutmegs.	½ pound citron.

Cream the butter and flour together, beat the yolks and sugar together, add the whites well beaten, mix them with the flour and butter. After this is all well beaten dredge fruit well with flour and put it in by degrees, add wine glass of whiskey or brandy. Bake in a loaf for four hours.

WHITE LADY CAKE.

12 eggs.	2½ teacups sugar.
1 teacup of butter.	3½ teacups of flour.
½ cup of cream.	3 teaspoonfuls baking powder.

Cream the butter and sugar together until very light; add the whites of eggs beaten stiff, then the flour, and then the baking powder stirred in the cream. Bake in a solid cake in a moderate oven for very nearly one hour. Any desired flavoring may be used.

LAYER CAKE.

1 cup butter.	6 eggs.
3 cups flour.	2 heaping teaspoons baking
½ cup milk.	powder.
2 cups sugar.	

Take only the whites of eggs, beaten stiff. Mix as in lady cake, and bake in tins in a moderate oven.

SPONGE CAKE.

| 12 eggs. | 1⅛ cups of sugar. |
| 1⅛ cups flour. | 1 level teaspoonful cream tartar. |

Beat the yolks of eight eggs with the sugar until very light. Beat the whites of twelve eggs with the cream tartar to a stiff froth. Add to the yolks and sugar, then add the flour slowly; flavor to taste, and bake in a moderate oven forty minutes.

ANGEL FOOD.

| 12 eggs, whites beaten stiff. | 1 teaspoonful cream tartar. |
| 1½ tumblers powdered sugar. | 1 tumbler of flour. |

Take the whites of eggs beaten to a stiff froth with the cream of tartar added. Sift the powdered sugar into the eggs and cut it in with an egg-beater (never stir angel food with a spoon.) After the flour has been sifted five times, sift very slowly into the egg and sugar. Add a teaspoonful of vanilla. Grease the cake pan very little with butter, lining the bottom with unglazed letter paper which has been slightly greased. Pour in the cake and bake forty minutes. Put a pan of water over it from the first. Remove from the oven, invert the pan, and let it stand until the cake falls out without being disturbed.

HICKORY NUT CAKE.

½ cup butter.	1 cup granulated sugar.
3 eggs.	1 cup milk.
1½ cups flour.	1½ teaspoons baking powder.
1 cup hickory nuts chopped fine.	

Cream the butter and add the sugar gradually. Beat the yolks of three eggs light and add to the butter and sugar with one cup milk. To the flour add the baking powder, stir into the batter, add the hickory nut meats chopped fine, and the whites of two eggs beaten stiff. Bake in a buttered and floured pan from forty to fifty minutes, or in small pans.

MOLASSES POUND CAKE.

⅔ cup butter.
¾ cup sugar.
2 eggs.
⅔ cup milk.
⅔ cup molasses.
2⅛ cups flour.

¾ teaspoon soda.
1 teaspoon cinnamon.
½ teasppon allspice.
¼ teaspoon clove.
¼ teaspoon mace.
½ cup seeded raisins, cut in pieces.

⅓ cup citron, thinly sliced and cut in strips.

Cream the butter, add sugar gradually, eggs well beaten, and milk and molasses. Mix and sift flour with soda and spices, and add to first mixture, then add fruit. Bake in small buttered tins from twenty-five to thirty minutes in a moderate oven. This recipe makes twenty-four little cakes.

CHOCOLATE COOKIES.

½ cup butter.
1 cup sugar.
1 egg.
¼ teaspoon salt.

2 ozs. unsweetened chocolate.
2½ cups flour (scant).
2 teaspoons baking powder.
¼ cup milk.

Cream the butter, add sugar gradually, egg well beaten, salt, and chocolate melted. Beat well, and add flour mixed and sifted with baking powder alternately with milk. Chill, roll very thin, then shape with a small cutter, first dipped in flour, and bake in a moderate oven.

PECAN MACAROONS.

Meat from 1 lb. pecans.   ¼ cup flour.
1 lb. powdered sugar.   Whites 6 eggs.
1 teaspoon vanilla.

Pound nut meat and mix with sugar and flour. Beat whites of eggs until stiff, add first mixture and vanilla. Drop from tip of tablespoon (allowing one spoonful for each cake) on a tin sheet covered with buttered paper. Bake twenty minutes in a moderate oven.

DEVIL'S FOOD.

Whites 8 eggs.   1 cup of butter.
3 cups sugar.   1 cup sweet or sour milk.
3 cups flour.   ½ cup grated chocolate melted.

Cream the butter and sugar together; add the chocolate, then the eggs. If sweet milk is used, use two teaspoons of baking powder. If buttermilk is used, use one teaspoon of soda. Whichever is used, add next to the mixture and lastly the flour. Bake in solid mold.

ICING.

Two cups of granulated sugar, one cup of brown sugar, three-fourths cup of grated chocolate, one cup rich cream, tablespoon of butter cooked until done; add vanilla and beat until it begins to thicken.

SPICE CAKE.

1 cup of sugar.   ½ cup of molasses.
½ cup of butter.   ½ cup of sour milk.
2½ cups of flour.   1 teaspoonful of soda.
1 tablespoonful cinnamon.   1 tablespoonful ginger.
4 eggs.   ½ teaspoonful of cloves.
½ teaspoonful allspice.   1½ pounds raisins (if desired).

Use only the well-beaten yolks of eggs. Bake in small pans or as a solid cake.

MUFFIN CAKES.

1 cup of butter.	3 cups of flour.
2 cups of sugar.	4 eggs.

Cream the butter and sugar together, beat eggs separately, add the yolks and then the whites. Dissolve two teaspoons of baking powder in one-half cup of milk, add to the batter, and lastly the flour. Bake in muffin rings.

BLACKBERRY JAM CAKE.

¾ cup of butter.	3 eggs.
1 cup of sugar.	1 cup of jam.
2 cups of flour.	3 tablespoons of cream.
2 teaspoons of cinnamon.	1 teaspoon baking powder.
1 teaspoon nutmeg.	1 teaspoon cloves.

1 teaspoon allspice.

Cream the butter and sugar, add the jam, then the eggs beaten separately, add the spices and then the baking powder dissolved in the cream, and lastly the flour. Bake in layers. Put white icing between and all over it.

SOUR MILK GINGER BREAD.

1 cup molasses.	1 cup sour milk.
2⅛ cups flour.	1¾ teaspoonfuls soda.
2 teaspoonfuls ginger.	½ teaspoonful salt.

¼ cup melted butter.

Add the milk to the molasses, mix and sift the dry ingredients, combine the two, add butter and beat vigorously. Pour into a buttered, shallow pan and bake twenty-five minutes in a moderate oven.

GINGER SNAPS.

2 cups molasses.	1 heaping teaspoon ginger.
1 cup of lard.	½ teaspoon pepper.
1 tablespoon of soda.	

Cream the molasses and lard together; add ginger and pepper, then dissolve the soda in as little hot water as possible and add flour enough to roll. Roll thin, cut out and bake in buttered pans with a little flour sprinkled over them.

GINGER SNAPS.

3 oz. sugar.	3 oz. butter.
¼ pint molasses.	⅛ pint water.
1 teaspoonful soda (level).	Ginger and cinnamon.
	12 oz. flour.

Take pieces the size of marbles, press flat on pan, wash over with water and bake in medium oven.

SUGAR CUBES.

4 oz. sugar.	4 oz. butter.
1 small egg.	8 oz. flour.

Lemon flavor, cut out, brush over top with milk, dip in granulated sugar and bake.

SPANISH BUNS.

Spanish buns can also be used for layer cakes.

12 oz. sugar.	8 oz. butter.
5 eggs.	½ pint milk.
2 teaspoonfuls baking powder.	1 pound flour.
	Lemon flavor.

Bake in greased and dusted muffin pans or layers.

ANGEL FOOD.

Beat the whites of eight eggs, gradually adding four ounces of sugar to keep whites from separating until very stiff, then add vanilla flavor, then mix in lightly four ounces sugar, four ounces flour, one-half teaspoonful cream tartar which has been sifted twice. Bake in a mould without being greased, turn over after leaving oven to steam when it will come out easily.

SUNSHINE CAKE.

Same as Angel Food only flavor with orange and vanilla and add yolks of eggs when beaten stiff before mixing in the other ingredients.

CHOCOLATE FEATHER CAKE.

Same as Angel Food cake only add two tablespoonfuls of cocoa with the ingredients. Vanilla flavor. Iced with chocolate icing.

GINGER BREAD. (Ten Portions.)

4 oz. lard.	4 oz. sugar.
1 egg.	½ pint molasses.
½ pint hot water.	Cinnamon, ginger and nutmeg
Rounded teaspoonful soda.	1 pound of flour.

Bake in medium oven.

WAFERS.

4 oz. sugar.	4 oz. butter.
2 eggs.	5 oz. flour.

Vanilla or lemon flavor.

Drop on slightly greased pans with teaspoon two inches apart. Bake in medium oven.

BRANDY SNAPS. (Scotch Cakes.)

4 oz. sugar.	2 oz. lard.
⅛ quart molasses.	4 oz. flour.

Roll in little balls the size of a marble, press on slightly greased pans two and half inches apart. Bake in medium oven until spread out clear.

GINGER CAKES.

4 oz. lard.	4 oz. sugar.
½ pint molasses.	3 tablespoonfuls milk.
1 pound flour.	Ginger, cinnamon and nutmeg.

Roll out on floured board and cut out with biscuit cutter and bake in medium hot oven.

LEMON SNAPS.

4 oz. sugar.	3 oz. butter.
7 oz. flour.	1 grated lemon.
Pinch of powdered ammonia.	1 large egg.

Mix the same as biscuit dough and add the egg as a binder, cut out with small biscuit cutter and put on slightly greased pans, one inch a-part, brush over top with part egg and water beaten together and bake in medium oven.

DRIED APPLE CAKE.

Two cups of dried apples, soaked in water an hour or two. Grind (medium) and cook with one cup of molasses until thick.

1 cup butter(or lard & butter).	2 teaspoons soda.
1 cup sugar (half brown).	3 eggs.
4 cups flour.	1 cup of sour milk.
2 teaspoons cinnamon, one of cloves.	

Add one cup of chopped nuts and two of raisins. Can be baked in loaf or muffins. Nuts, cherries or citron may be used to decorate.

GINGER BREAD.

1 cup molasses.	⅛ cup of butter.
1¾ teaspoonfuls soda.	½ cup sour milk.
1 egg.	2 cups flour.
2 teaspoonfuls ginger.	½ teaspoonful of salt.

Put the butter and molasses in a saucepan and cook until the boiling point is reached. Remove from the fire, add the soda and beat vigorously, then add the milk, eggs well beaten, and the remaining ingredients mixed and sifted. Bake fifteen minutes in buttered pans two-thirds filled with the mixture.

COOKIES.

3 cups sugar.	1½ cups butter.
6 eggs.	5 pints flour.
3 teaspoonfuls carbonate of ammonia.	

Cream the butter and sugar, beat the eggs three at a time into it, and then beat well. Add the ammonia, and lastly flour, and roll thin.

SAND TARTS.

1 cup butter.	2 cups sugar.
3 eggs.	Flour enough to roll.

Roll thin, paint the tops with the white of egg, sprinkle over with equal parts of ground cinnamon and granulated sugar, and in the center of each place one-fourth of a blanched almond. Put in floured pans and bake in a quick oven.

CRULLERS.

2 cups of butter.	3½ cups of sugar.
12 eggs.	Flour enough to roll.

Flavor with nutmeg or cinnamon, roll thin, shape and fry in hot fat.

MOLASSES SAUCE.

1 cup molasses.	2 tablespoons lemon juice or
1½ tablespoons butter.	1 tablespoon vinegar.

Boil molasses and butter five minutes; remove from fire and add lemon juice. Fine with ginger bread.

NURRUMBURGHS.

2 eggs.	⅓ teaspoon ground cinnamon.
½ cup sugar.	⅛ teaspoon ground cloves.
¾ cup flour.	⅔ cup roasted almonds.
¼ teaspoon salt.	1 tablespoon candied orange peel.
	Grated rind of ½ of lemon.

Beat whites of two eggs stiff, add one cup of sugar and yolks of two eggs, three-fourths cup of flour, one-fourth teaspoon salt, one-third teaspoon cinnamon, one-eighth teaspoon cloves, two-thirds cup roasted almonds. Drop on sheet sprinkled with one-half sugar and one-half corn starch. Sprinkle top with chopped almonds, cut out and bake.

FILLINGS FOR CAKES.

PLAIN CARAMEL.

2 cups of sugar.	¾ cup of maple syrup.
Cream to wet throughly.	1 tablespoonful butter.

Put sugar, syrup and cream on, and when it boils add the butter. Boil it until very thick. Add one teaspoonful of vanilla, take from the fire, and beat until it begins to sugar. Then pour over the cake.

CHOCOLATE CARAMEL.

Same as above, only before it begins to boil add one-fourth cake of Wilbur's chocolate.

SOUR CREAM FILLING.

Blanch one-half pound almonds and chop them. Beat a teacup of sour cream until light and thick; add three tablespoonfuls of sugar, two eggs beaten separately, and the chopped nuts. Hickory or any kind of nuts can be used. Spread between layers of cake.

ICE CREAM FILLING.

3 cups sugar.	1 cup water.
3 eggs, whites beaten stiff.	1 teaspoonful vanilla.

Boil sugar and water to a candy, pour slowly over the beaten whites of three eggs, flavor with vanilla, beat until it begins to cream, and pour over the cake.

Grated cocoanut sprinkled between the layers and on top makes a delicious cocoanut cake.

Blanched almonds grated and mixed with the icing makes a delicious filling.

MARSHMALLOW AND PINEAPPLE FILLING.

Take fresh marshmallows, put into the oven to soften, spread over the cake with a little chopped candied pine-apple, and pour over same the ice cream filling given above.

CREAM ICING FOR ANGEL FOOD.

3 cups of sugar.   ½ teaspoonful of vanilla.   1 cup of cream.

Let it come to a good hard boil, beat hard until creamy and pour over the angel food.

PRAULINE ICING.

Make a plain caramel, and when done add one cup of broken pecan kernels just before pouring on the cake.

ICES

NESSELBRODE PUDDING.

1 cup of marons.	1 cup of granulated sugar.
Yolks of 3 eggs.	½ pint of cream.
¼ pound of candied fruits.	½ can pineapple (drained).

Take candied fruits and marons and soak them in sherry wine. Put sugar on the fire with one-fourth of a cup of boiling water and boil to a syrup. Beat the yolks of eggs until light. Pour on them slowly the syrup, stirring all the time. Put on the fire in a double boiler and cook until the consistency of thick cream. Remove and beat hard until cold. When cold, add the cream, the marons pounded, and half a teaspoonful of vanilla, and freeze. When nearly hard frozen, add the candied fruits, one-fourth of a pound of raisins, one-fourth of a pound of pounded almonds, and a glass of sherry wine, and freeze hard. Remove the dasher and allow it to stand for several hours.—*Century Cook Book.*

PLAIN VANILLA CREAM.

Take one quart of plain, rich cream, season and flavor. When half frozen, add one quart of stiff whipped cream which has been sweetened and flavored. Freeze hard. Pack for an hour before using.

SULTANA ROLL.

Line a mold with pistachio ice cream, sprinkle with Sultana raisins, fill center with whipped cream, and let stand two and one-half hours. Pack in ice and salt. Serve with claret sauce.

PISTACHIO ICE CREAM.

Scald one pint of cream. Mix one tablespoon of flour, one cup of sugar, one-fourth teaspoon salt, and one beaten egg; pour on one pint of milk; cook twenty minutes in double boiler, stirring often. Cool. Add one quart of cream flavored with one tablespoon of vanilla, tablespoon of almonds. Strain and freeze. Use just enough of Burnett's Fruit Coloring to make a pretty green.

CLARET SAUCE.

Boil one cup sugar and one-third cup water to a syrup. Cool and add five tablespoonfuls claret.

TO FREEZE A WATERMELON.

Take three pints of stiff whipped cream, color with Burnett's Green Vegetable Coloring, sweeten and flavor with extract of pistachio, put in a freezer and freeze very hard.

Then take a quart of very stiff whipped cream, sweeten and flavor with a little sherry wine, put in a freezer and freeze hard.

Then take a quart of stiff whipped cream, sweeten and color pink with Burnett's Vegetable Coloring, and flavor with strawberry. Put in a freezer and freeze hard.

Take a melon mold and line it with the green, then put a layer of the white, and then the pink, sprinkled well with Sultana raisins that have been soaked in brandy, making the seeds. Cover with the white cream, and then the green; put a piece of buttered letter paper over it and then the tin top. Pack in salt and ice, and let stand for several hours.

FROZEN APRICOTS.

Cut one can of apricots in small pieces, drain and add to the syrup water enough to make a quart, add one and one-half cups of sugar and cook ten minutes. Cool—partially freeze—add apricots and finish freezing. Pack the freezer with crushed ice and rock salt in proportions of three to one.

THREE OF A KIND.

Juice of 3 lemons.   Juices of 3 oranges.
Sugar to taste.   3 slices of canned peaches or
2 bananas.   pineapple.
1 quart of cold water.

Take the lemon juice, cold water and sugar and a pint of rich cream to be added after the lemon and water are packed in the freezer. When this begins to freeze, add the juice of three oranges, two bananas which have been put through a fine sieve, and three slices of canned peaches or pineapple put through a sieve. Freeze until very hard. Pack and serve.

VICTORIA PUNCH.

Boil three and one-half cups water and two cups sugar fifteen minutes. Add the juice of four lemons and grated rind and juice of two oranges. Cool and partially freeze. Add one cup angelica, one cup cider, one and one-half tablespoonfuls gin and freeze again. Alcoholic liquors retard freezing.

HOLLANDAISE PUNCH.

4 cups of water.   1⅓ cups of sugar.
⅛ cup of lemon juice.   1 can pineapple.
¼ cup of brandy.   2 tablespoonfuls of gin.

Cook the water, sugar and a little grated lemon rind fifteen minutes. Add lemon juice and pineapple, cool, strain and freeze partly, then add the liquor and continue freezing.

GRAPE FRUIT SHERBET.

To one cup boiling water add three-fourths cup sugar and let boil one minute. Cool, add two cups grape fruit juice, one tablespoon lemon juice and a few grains salt. Freeze, using one part rock salt to three parts ice. Do not let grape fruit stand long before using.

ORANGE DELICIOUS.

2 cups sugar.	1 cup cream.
1 cup water.	Yolks two eggs.
2 cups orange juice.	1 cup heavy cream.

¼ cup shredded candied orange peel.

Boil sugar and water eight minutes, then add orange juice. Scald cream, add yolks of eggs, and cook over hot water until mixture thickens. Cool, add to first mixture with heavy cream beaten stiff. Freeze; when nearly frozen, add orange peel. Line a melon mould with Orange Ice, fill with Orange Delicious, pack in salt and ice, and let stand one and one-half hours.

MAPLE PARFAIT.

4 eggs.	1 cup hot maple syrup.

1 pint thick cream.

Beat eggs slightly, and pour on slowly maple syrup. Cook until mixture thickens, cool, and add cream beaten until stiff. Mould, pack in salt and ice, and let stand three hours.

PLOMBIERE GLACE.

Cover the bottom of small paper cases with vanilla ice cream, sprinkle ice cream with marron glace broken in pieces, arrange lady fingers at equal distances, and allow them to extend one inch above cases. Pile whipped cream sweetened and flavored, in the center and garnish with marron glace and candied violets or glace cherries.

FROZEN PLUM PUDDING.

1 cup milk.	2½ cups cream.
1 cup sugar.	¾ cup candied fruit.
Yolks 6 eggs.	½ cup almonds, blanched and
¼ teaspoon salt.	chopped.
¼ cup sherry.	⅛ cup Sultana raisins.

½ cup pounded macaroons.

Make custard of milk, one-half the sugar, egg yolks, and salt. Carmelize the remaining sugar and add. Strain, cool, add remaining ingredients, freeze, and mould.

MONTROSE PUDDING.

1 cup of cream.	Yolks of 6 eggs.
1 cup of granulated sugar.	Vanilla.

Put a pint of cream on in a double boiler, and when hot add eggs and sugar. Cook until it thickens. Remove from the fire, add vanilla, and when cold, add one *pint of cream whipped*. When partially frozen line a mold and fill the center with raspberry, pineapple or orange sherbet.

SAUCE.

1 tablespoon of gelatine.	Yolks of 3 eggs.
¼ cup of powdered sugar.	1 tablespoon of vanilla.
1 pint of cream.	2 tablespoons brandy and sherry wine.

Dissolve the gelatine in a little hot water. Add the yolks of the eggs; add the sugar and the cream. Boil to a syrup. When it begins to thicken add the gelatine; remove from fire, and when cold add the vanilla, brandy and sherry wine.

ORANGE ICE.

To four cups of sugar add a quart of water, and boil to a thick syrup. Add to this the juice of twelve oranges and four lemons, and one quart of cold water. Put in a freezer and freeze. Pineapple or any water ice may be made in the same way.

FRUIT PUNCH.

Take the same syrup as above; add one quart of sherry, one-half pint of brandy, one-half pint of rum, one pound of candied cherries, one-half pound candied pineapple, half a pound of grapes, and the juice of six lemons with the extra quart of cold water.

FRENCH ICE CREAM.

Scald two cups milk with one-half cup sugar and one-half inch piece cut from a vanilla bean. Beat yolks six eggs slightly, add one-third cup sugar and one-fourth teaspoon salt. Combine mixtures and cook in double boiler until mixture thickens. Strain, cool and add one pint cream; then freeze.

FRUIT ICE CREAM.

One-half gallon fresh chopped peaches or fresh strawberries, sweetened to taste. Let stand in sugar over night or for several hours. Add one-half gallon sweet cream and freeze.

FRUIT SAUCE.

One cup of sugar, one half-cup of water boiled to a syrup, add fruit juice and boil until thick. If desired, add one-half cup of whipped cream and serve cold, on cream or sherbet.

CHOCOLATE SAUCE.

1 cup of boiling water.   6 tablespoons of grated chocolate.
½ cup of sugar.   ½ cup of milk.
                ½ tablespoon of arrowroot.

Boil the water and sugar; add the chocolate moistened with one-half cup of milk, and the arrowroot dissolved in one-half cup of water; boil three minutes.   Strain and serve hot or cold, on ice cream or cake.

Grape juice is delicious served over sherbet.

NUT CARAMEL SAUCE FOR ICE CREAM.

One cup of maple syrup, one cup of sugar boiled until thick.   Add one-half cup of nut kernels chopped fine, or if more nuts are desired, add whole cup.

BRANDY SAUCE FOR ICE CREAM.

One cup of sugar and one cup of water boiled until thick.   When cold add three tablespoons of brandy, or more if desired, and add one cup of whipped cream.

MISCELLANEOUS

COFFEE.

One cup of coffee (ground), one egg, one cup of cold water, six cups of boiling water. Scald coffee pot. Beat egg slightly, dilute with one-half the cold water, add crushed shell and mix with coffee. Turn into coffee pot and pour on boiling water, and stir throughly. Place on front of range and boil three minutes. If not boiled, coffee is cloudy. If boiled too long, too much tannic acid is developed. Stir and pour some in a cup to be sure spout is free from grounds. Return to coffee pot and repeat. Add remaining cold water, which perfects clearing. Cold water being heavier than hot, sinks to the bottom, carrying grounds with it. Place on back of range for ten minutes where it will not boil. Serve at once.

PASTRY CRULLERS.

1 quart flour.	2 cups water.
2 eggs.	1 tablespoonful of butter.

Mix the flour and water, then the butter, then the beaten eggs and a little salt. Have the cruller iron heated thoroughly in boiling lard. Be very careful to drain all the lard from the iron, dip into some of the batter which you have put into a pint cup, being careful not to let the iron touch the bottom or sides of the cup; then dip in boiling lard and fry to a nice brown; remove from the iron and heat it again. Serve plain this way as a garnish, or sprinkle with cinnamon sugar as a cruller.

CHOCOLATE.

1½ squares Wilbur's chocolate.   Few grains salt.
4 tablespoons sugar.   1 cup boiling water.
3 cups milk and cream.

Scald milk and cream.   Melt chocolate in small sauce-pan placed over hot water, add sugar, salt and gradually boiling water; when smooth, place on range and boil one minute; add to scalded milk and cream; mill, and serve in chocolate cups with whipped cream.   One and one-half ounces vanilla chocolate may be substituted for Wilbur's chocolate; being sweetened, less sugar is required.

QUEEN FRITTERS.

One quarter (scant) cup of butter, one-half cup of boiling water, one-half cup of flour, two eggs.   Put butter in small saucepan, and pour on water.   As soon as the water reaches boiling point add flour all at once, and stir until mixture leaves sides of saucepan.   Remove from fire and add eggs unbeaten, one at a time, beating mixture thoroughly between eggs.   Drop by spoonfuls and fry in deep fat until well browned.   Drain, make an opening and fill with preserves or fresh fruits.   Sprinkle with sugar.

APPLE FRITTERS.

1 cup of flour.   ⅔ cup of water.
1 tablespoon sugar.   ½ tablespoon olive oil or Snow-
¼ teaspoon salt.   flake oil.
White of 1 egg.   2 medium sized sour apples.

Mix flour, sugar and salt, add water gradually; then oil and white of egg beaten until stiff.   Peel, core, and cut apples in eighths; then cut eighths in slices and stir into batter.   Drop by spoonfuls and fry in deep fat. Drain on brown paper and sprinkle with powdered sugar.   Serve hot.

SWEDISH TIMBALS.

One pint of flour less two tablespoonfuls, one-half pint sweet milk, three eggs, two tablespoonfuls olive oil or Snowflake oil, one teaspoonful of salt. Stir flour and milk to perfectly smooth batter, add oil, then salt and eggs. Dip timbal iron in boiling oil, then in batter, and then in fat, fill with fricasseed oysters with mushrooms.

OMELET.

4 eggs.	½ teaspoon salt.
4 tablespoons milk.	⅛ teaspoon pepper.
2 tablespoon butter.	

Beat eggs slightly, just enough to blend yolks and whites, add the milk and seasonings. Put butter in hot omelet pan; when melted, turn in the mixture; as it cooks, prick and pick up with a fork until the whole is of creamy consistency. Place on hotter part of range that it may brown quickly underneath. Fold, and turn on hot platter.

SPANISH OMELET.

Mix and cook omelet. Serve with Tomato Sauce in the center and around omelet.

TOMATO SAUCE.

Cook two tablespoons of butter with one tablespoon of finely chopped onion, until yellow. Add one and three-fourths cups tomatoes, and cook until moisture has nearly evaporated. Add one tablespoon sliced mushrooms, one tablespoon capers, one-fourth teaspoon salt, and a few grains cayenne. A little chopped red or green pepper.

CREAM CHICKEN.

½ boiled chicken.	1 pint of cream.
1 tablespoon of butter.	½ cup green peppers.
1 tablespoon of flour.	Salt, pepper and celery.
Sauce to taste.	

Melt one tablespoon of butter, add one tablespoon of flour, and when thoroughly blended add the cream and seasonings. Cook until thick, and add one-half chicken which has been put through a meat grinder and one-half cup of green peppers which have been parboiled and cut fine. Serve on buttered toast or patty shell.

EGG TIMBALS.

Seven eggs. Beat yolks and whites (separately) very light. Then mix together, add one cup cream, salt and pepper to taste. Put in well buttered molds and set in pan of hot water in the oven for a little while. Turn out of molds on a hot platter and pour a rich white sauce over them. A delicious breakfast or luncheon dish.

SCRAMBLED EGGS, SAN JUAN.

Mince two green peppers, two sweet red peppers and fry in butter ten minutes, add one tomato peeled and quartered, salt and tabasco sauce. Let simmer ten minutes more. Scramble six eggs and mix the above preparation with them. Serve on toast with a tomato sauce around them.

EGG NOG.

12 eggs.   12 tablespoonfuls of sugar.
12 tablespoonfuls best whiskey. 12 tablespoonfuls Jamaica rum.

Beat the yolks and sugar together until very light; then add the liquor slowly, next the whites, beaten to a stiff froth, and then one pint and a half of cream, whipped.

CHEESE RAMEQUINES.

Mix one-half cup of grated cheese (mild), one tablespoon flour, one-half saltspoon of salt, and a little cayenne pepper; add the well-beaten whites of three eggs. Shape in balls, allowing three tablespoonsful for each ball, and fry in hot fat.

SALTED ALMONDS.

Blanch the almonds, wipe dry, place in a frying-basket, then into Snowflake oil, heated to the boiling point. When nicely browned, remove from the oil, sprinkle salt on them and let them drain. Any other nut can be cooked in the same way.

FRUIT SALAD.

Equal quantities of green grapes, oranges, pineapples, grape fruit, maraschino, or candied cherries all cut up together and serve with sherry. This is delicious frozen and used as first course. The grapes and pineapples sweetened and frozen together with plenty of sherry make a delicious first course also.

A DAINTY FIRST COURSE.

Fill tall glass half full of maraschino or creme de menthe cherries. Put lemon or pineapple sherbet on top. Garnish with fresh mint.

ANCHOVY EGGS.

Cut hard-boiled eggs in two, lengthwise. (Boil the eggs twenty-five minutes, so that the yolks will be thoroughly done). Take out the yolks. Mash them well, mix them with mayonnaise dressing and the trimmings of the anchovies. Fill the one-half with the mixture, covering the whole top. Trim anchovies to the right length and lay two of them across the top of each. To make it stand firm, slice a little piece from the bottom of the egg. Garnish with parsley and serve as first course.

MOLASSES TAFFY.

2 cups of brown sugar.	1 tablespoon butter.
¾ cup of molasses.	2 teaspoons of vanilla.

¼ cup water.

Boil the sugar, molasses, and water until when dropped in a little cold water you can pick it up in your fingers. Then add butter and cook until candy is brittle when trying it in the water. Add the vanilla. Pour on buttered pans and pull. Be careful not to stir, or it will turn to sugar. When first put on to boil, a bit of cream of tartar will add to the lightness of it.

ICE CREAM CANDY.

2 cups of granulated or powdered sugar.	2 tablespoons of vinegar.
	1 tablespoon of butter.
1 cup of water.	2 tablespoons of vanilla.

Cook the same as molasses candy.

CHEESE SOUFFLE.

Melt two tablespoons butter, add three tablespoons flour and stir until well blended; then pour on gradually, while stirring constantly, one-half cup milk. Add one-fourth cup grated young America cheese, one-half teaspoon salt and a few grains cayenne. Add the yolks of three eggs beaten until thick and lemon-colored, and cut and fold in the whites of three eggs beaten until stiff and dry. Cook in chafing-dish until firm.

CHEESE CROQUETTES.

Grate half a pound of American cheese. Mix in it a scant tablespoonful of butter, a tablespoonful of milk, an egg beaten enough to break it, half a teaspoonful of salt, and a dash of paprika. Mix to a smooth paste and mold into small croquettes, using a tablespoonful of the paste for each croquette. The above proportions will make eight croquettes.

Add a little milk to the yolk of an egg and roll the croquettes in this and then in cracker dust. Then fry them for a minute in smoking hot fat. They should have a delicate brown color and be soft inside. Serve them as soon as they are fried, or the cheese will harden.

This is a delicious cheese dish and very easily made.

CHILI CON CARNI.

2 cans of tomatoes.	1 lemon minus the juice.
1 stalk of celery.	1 tablespoon of whole cloves.
9 red pepper pods.	1 tablespoon of whole allspice.
5 dried onions.	2 quarts of water.
	3 pods of garlic.

Boil hard for two hours. Strain through colander. Put on at the same time two pounds of Hamburg steak in a little water; boil for two hours; add to this three cans of kidney beans. Add these to the tomatoes. Then add two tablespoons of Chili powder and serve hot. Enough for two meals for family of six.

CARAMELS.

1½ pounds of brown sugar.	¼ pound of Wilbur's chocolate.
½ pound of butter.	1 cup of cream or milk.

Put in kettle and boil until, when tried in cold water, a firm ball may be held in the fingers.

NUT CARAMELS.

1 cup of chocolate.	1½ pounds of almonds blanched
1 pound of meat of English walnut.	and chopped.

BUTTER SCOTCH.

1 cup of sugar.	1 tablespoon vinegar.
¼ cup of molasses.	2 tablespoons of boiling water.

½ cup of butter.

Boil the ingredients until, when tried in cold water, the mixture will be brittle. Flavor with vanilla. Pour into a well-buttered pan, and when cool, cut in squares.

RAISIN PICKLES.

2 pounds of raisins.	2 teaspoons white mustard.
3 dozen cucumbers (sliced).	2 teaspoons of celery.
Piece of stick cinnamon.	1 teaspoon black pepper.
3 teaspoons mace.	3 coffee cups brown sugar.

1 quart of vinegar.

Put on the vinegar, spices, and sugar, and when it boils put in the raisins and let boil until clear. Pour all over the cucumbers which are ready in a vessel large enough to mix altogether. If fresh cucumbers are used, soak in salt water over night. If pickled cucumbers are used, chop and add.

CUCUMBER PICKLE.

4 dozen cucumbers.   4 dozen onions.   24 green peppers.

Cut each cucumber in four pieces, scoop out the seeds and chop cucumber. Slice the onions and chop up the green peppers. Put all together in a bag. Put over them one quart of salt, tablespoon of celery seed, tablespoon allspice, one-half tablespoon cloves and let stand over night. The same day take five quarts of vinegar made very sweet with sugar. Boil and let stand over night. The next morning take the pickles out of the bag and put in jar. Pour over the five quarts of vinegar, and they are ready for use. This is delicious served with game or fish. Very pretty served in a half lemon scooped out.

GREEN TOMATO SWEET PICKLE.

One gallon of sliced green tomatoes, sprinkled with salt and let stand two days. Pour off all the water and add

2 tablespoonfuls of whole cloves.	3 tablespoonfuls of whole allspice.
1 tablespoonful of whole black pepper.	1 tablespoonful of whole mace.
	1 small cup mustard seed.
2 tablespoonfuls of whole celery. seed.	1½ pounds of brown sugar.
	6 small onions sliced.

Cover all with vinegar and boil until tender. If vinegar is very sour, more sugar may be needed.

SPANISH PICKLE.

2 dozen cucumbers large, or 4 dozen small.	½ dozen large green peppers.
	2 dozen white onions sliced.
½ peck of green tomatoes.	½ peck green beans.
1 cup of sugar.	

Cut the cucumbers in slices one inch thick, slice tomatoes thin and sprinkle with salt and let stand twenty-four hours. Then rinse off the salt. Grate two roots of horseradish, add one-fourth pound of white mustard seed and five red peppers cut up. One ounce stick cinnamon. Make a paste of one pound of mustard, one ounce of celery seed, one ounce of turmeric, one pint Snowflake or olive oil.

Put vegetables in a pan and mix spices and paste all through them, scald enough vinegar (one gallon or more) to cover them. Pour over boiling hot. Stir every day or two. Ready for use in about two weeks. Makes three gallons.

GRAPE PICKLE.

7 pounds of grapes.	1 pint of vinegar.
3½ pounds of sugar.	1 oz. of cloves.
1 oz. ground cinnamon.	

Pulp the grapes and boil until the seeds can be strained out through a sieve; then put the skins and all into the syrup and boil fifteen minutes or longer. Tie spices in a bag.

GREEN TOMATO PICKLE.

Slice a peck of small green tomatoes thin and half as many nice onions. Place them in layers in a stone jar. Sprinkle each layer very lightly with salt. Weight them down for twelve hours, then let them drain (I put mine in separate jars or bags). Put in a porcelain kettle, sprinkle through them one-half pound white mustard seed. In a bowl put

2 pounds of sugar.	1 heaping tablespoon cinnamon.
1 teaspoon mace (heaping).	1 heaping tablespoon ginger.
1 teaspoon allspice.	1 heaping tablespoon black pepper
1 teaspoon cloves.	2 tablespoons of celery seed.

Mix all of these ingredients with a little cold vinegar until smooth, then add a gallon more. Turn over the tomatoes with some strips of horseradish; stew slowly and stir often with a wooden spoon to prevent burning. Ready for use as soon as cold. This is good either sliced or chopped.

BANANA CROQUETTES.

Remove the skin and coarse threads from the banana and trim pulp of each to a long croquette. Roll in an egg beaten with a teaspoonful of cold water and then in bread crumbs seasoned with salt and pepper. Fry one-half minute in hot fat. Drain on soft paper.

BRANDY PEACHES.

Peel and weigh the peaches and put to them about half the weight of sugar. Put in the kettle just enough water to moisten the sugar and let boil until the peaches are done enough to pierce to the seed with a straw. Then take them out and put on dishes. Boil syrup until it is quite thick. Then put in a bowl to cool. To three pints of syrup add two pints of whiskey or brandy, and pour it over the peaches in air-tight jars.

EGGS BAKED IN TOMATOES.

Select round tomatoes of uniform size. Cut off the stem ends and take out enough of the pulp to leave a space as large as an egg. Sprinkle the inside with salt and pepper. Drop into each one an egg. Place the filled tomatoes in a baking-dish with a little hot water, and bake them about fifteen minutes, or until the eggs are set and the tomatoes are a little softened. Serve the eggs on rounds of bread browned in butter. No sauce is required with this dish.

BOILED HAM.

Soak several hours or over night in cold water to cover. Wash thoroughly, trim off hard skin near end of bone, put in a kettle, cover with cold water, heat to boiling point, and cook slowly until tender. Remove kettle from range and set aside, that ham may partially cool; then take from water, remove outside skin, sprinkle with sugar and fine cracker crumbs, and stick with cloves one-half inch apart. Bake one hour in a slow oven. Serve cold, thinly sliced. Boil four to five hours.

OATMEAL WITH SLICED BANANAS.

Have the water salty—one-half teaspoon to a pint of freshly boiled water. Stir in slowly one cup of steam-cooked oats to two cups of water. Let boil up once after all the grain is added. Then set into hot water kettle or double boiler and cook from one-half hour to a full hour; the latter is preferable. Pour into patent charlotte russe molds or cups and let it stand over night. In the morning turn from the molds into a hot baking sheet and set in the oven until very hot. If molded in cups remove the centers, leaving a wall of the oatmeal. Remove to the serving dishes with a broad-bladed knife and fill the centers with slices of banana. Put a spoonful of whipped cream above the bananas, and serve in a nest of whipped cream.

HOW TO MAKE TEA.

3 teaspoons tea.   2 cups boiling water.

Scald an earthen or china teapot. Put in tea, and pour on boiling water. Let stand on back of range or in a warm place five minutes. Strain and serve immediately, with or without sugar and milk. Avoid second steeping of leaves with addition of a few fresh ones. If this is done, so large an amount of tannin is extracted that various ills are apt to follow.

RUSSIAN TEA.

Follow recipe for making tea. Russian tea may be served hot or cold, but always without milk. A thin slice of lemon, from which seeds have been removed, or a few drops of lemon juice, is allowed for each cup. Sugar is added according to taste. In Russia a preserved strawberry to each cup is considered an improvement. We imitate our Russian friends by garnishing with a candied cherry.

APPLE BUTTER.

½ bushel of apples (sliced thin).   ⅓ gallon sugar.

Place in layers in vessel to be cooked in. Set over night. Cover close and cook without stirring until done. Then stir well, flavor to taste and is ready for use.

TOMATO RELISH.

1 pint of ripe tomatoes.   3 onions.
1½ teaspoons of salt.   3 green peppers.

Chop tomatoes, onions and peppers fine, drain twenty-four or forty-eight hours. Sweeten one quart of vinegar with one quart of sugar, one ounce celery seed, one ounce white mustard seed. Do not cook.

SIMPLE DISHES FOR THE SICK

TOAST WATER.

Toast three slices of stale bread to a dark brown, but do not burn. Put into a pitcher, pour over them one quart boiling water. Cover closely and let stand on ice until cold. Strain. If desired, wine and sugar may be added.

RICE WATER.

Pick over and wash two tablespoonfuls of rice. Put into a granite saucepan with one quart boiling water. Simmer two hours, when rice should be softened and partially dissolved. Strain; add a saltspoonful of salt. Serve warm or cold. Two tablespoonfuls of sherry or port may be added if desired.

BARLEY WATER.

Wash two ounces (one wineglassful) of pearl barley with cold water. Boil five minutes in fresh water. Throw both waters away; pour on two quarts of boiling water and boil down to one quart. Flavor with thinly cut lemon rind. Add sugar to taste. Do not strain unless at the patient's request.

EGG WATER.

Stir the whites of two eggs into half a pint of ice water without beating the eggs. Add enough salt or sugar to make palatable.

FLAXSEED TEA.

Flaxseed, whole, 1 oz. (1 heap- White sugar, 1 oz.
    ing tablespoonful).   Lemon juice, 4 tablespoonfuls.
    Licorice root, ½ oz. (two small sticks).

Pour on these materials two pints of boiling water. Let stand in a hot place four hours and strain off the liquor.

PEPTONIZED MILK (Cold Process).

In a clean quart bottle put one peptonizing powder (extract of pancreas 5 grains, bicarbonate of soda 15 grains —or the contents of one peptonizing tube—Fairchild), add one teacup of cold water and shake well. Add one pint of fresh cold milk and shake mixture again. Place on ice. Use when required without subjecting to heat.

PEPTONIZED MILK (Warm Process).

Mix peptonizing powder with water and milk as described above; place bottle in water only so hot that the whole hand can be held in it a minute without discomfort Keep the bottle there ten minutes. Then put on ice to check further digestion. Do not heat long enough to render the milk bitter.

PEPTONIZED MILK TOAST.

Over two slices of toast pour one gill of peptonized milk (cold process), let stand on the back of stove thirty minutes, serve warm or strain and serve fluid portion alone. Plain, light sponge cake may be similarly digested.

KOUMISS.

Take ordinary beer bottle with shifting cork, put in it one pint of milk, one-sixth of a cake of Fleischmann's yeast, or one tablespoonful of fresh lager beer yeast (brewer's), one-half of a tablespoonful of white sugar reduced to a syrup. Shake well and allow it to stand in the refrigerator two or three days, when it may be used. It will keep there indefinitely if laid on its side. Much waste can be saved by preparing the bottles with ordinary corks wired in position, and drawing off the koumiss with a champagne tap.

CREAMED OATMEAL.

Boil oatmeal as for breakfast, rub it through a fine sieve, add a little cream, and cook very slowly in a double boiler for half an hour longer. When perfectly smooth, add a very little salt and rich cream. This is the most delicate preparation of oatmeal that an invalid can take.

CREAMED SWEETBREADS.

Make sauce as for cream chicken (on page 153). Add parboiled sweetbreads chopped fine and a tablespoonful of sherry wine.

PANNED OYSTERS.

Put two tablespoonfuls of butter in a saute pan. Lay twenty good-sized oysters into it. When the edges curl and the oysters plump, dust them with pepper and salt, and serve at once on toast. Two tablespoonfuls of sherry can be added before serving if desired.

RAW MEAT DIET.

Scrape pulp from a good steak; season to taste. Spread on slices of bread, then sear the bread slightly, and serve as a sandwich.

APPLE SOUP.

Two cups of raw apple, two cups of water, two tea-spoonfuls of corn starch, one and a half tablespoonfuls of sugar, one saltspoonful of cinnamon, and a bit of salt. Stew the apple in the water until it is very soft.   Then mix together in a smooth paste the corn starch, sugar, salt and cinnamon with a little cold water. Pour this into the apple and boil five minutes. Strain it and keep hot until ready to serve. May serve with cream if desired.

BEEF MINCE.

Have a pound of beef from the round.   Free it from all sinews and fat.   Mince it very fine.   To two table-spoonfuls of butter in a saucepan put in the meat and a teaspoonful of onion juice.   Stir for three or four minutes, or until the meat is hot through.   Add salt and pepper, and if desired a little lemon juice.   Serve on hot buttered toast.

FLAXSEED LEMONADE.

One tablespoonful of whole flaxseed, one pint of boiling water, lemon juice and sugar.   Pick over and wash the flaxseed, add water, and cook two hours, keeping just below the boiling point. Strain; add lemon juice and sugar to taste.

ORANGEADE.

Juice of 1 orange.   1½ tablespoonfuls of syrup.
2 tablespoonfuls of crushed ice.

Make a syrup by boiling eight minutes one cup of water and half a cup of sugar.   Mix the orange juice and the syrup and pour over the crushed ice.

SHERRY NOG.

To the yolk of one egg thoroughly beaten add one tablespoonful of powdered sugar and two tablespoonfuls of sherry wine and a pint of whipped cream.

MILK PUNCH.

½ cup milk.   Sugar.
1 tablespoon whisky, rum or   Few gratings nutmeg.
    brandy.

Mix ingredients, cover and shake well.

COCOA CORDIAL.

1 teaspoon cocoa.   ½ cup boiling water.
1 teaspoon sugar.   1½ tablespoons port wine.

Mix cocoa and sugar, add enough of the water to form a paste. Stir in remainder of water and boil one minute, then add wine. Useful in cases of chill or exhaustion.

PEPTONIZED OYSTERS.

Mince six large or twelve small oysters. Add to them, in their own liquor, five grains of extract of pancreas with fifteen grains bicarbonate of soda, or one Fairchild peptonizing tube. The mixture is then brought to a blood heat and maintained, with occasional stirring, at that temperature thirty minutes, when one pint of milk is added and the temperature kept up ten to twenty minutes. Finally the mass is brought to a boiling point; strain and serve. Gelatine may be added and the mixture served cold as a jelly. Cooked tomatoes, onions, celery or other flavoring suited to individual tastes may be added at the beginning of artificial digestion.

BEEF TEA.

Free a pound of lean beef from fat, tendon, cartilage, bone and vessels; chop up fine, put into a pint of cold water for two hours. Simmer on the stove three hours, but do not boil. Make up for the water lost by adding cold water so that a pint of beef tea represents one pound of beef. Press the beef very carefully, and strain.

BEEF JUICE.

Cut a thin, juicy steak into pieces about one and one-half inches square. Sear separately one and one-half minutes, on each side, over a hot fire. Squeeze in a hot lemon squeezer, flavor with salt and pepper. May add to milk or pour on toast.

MEAT CURE.

Procure slices of steak from the top of the round, without fat. Cut meat into strips, removing all fat, gristle, etc., with a knife. Put meat through mincer at least twice. Then beat it well in a roomy saucepan with cold water or skimmed beef tea, to the consistency of cream. The right proportion is one teaspoonful of liquid to eight of pulp. Add black pepper and salt to taste. Stir the mince briskly with a wooden spoon the whole time it is cooking, over a slow fire, or on the cool part of cupboard range, until hot through and through and the red color disappears. This requires one and one-half hours. When done it should be a soft, stiff, smooth puree, of the consistency of good paste. Serve hot. Add for the first few meals a softly poached white of an egg.

STERILIZED MILK.

Put the required amount of milk in clean bottles; if
for infants, each bottle holding enough for one feeding.
Plug the mouths lightly with rubber stoppers, immerse
to the shoulders in a kettle of cold water. Boil twenty
minutes, or better steam thirty minutes in ordinary steam-
er. Push in the stoppers firmly, cool the bottles rapidly
and keep in a refrigerator. Warm each bottle just before
using.

BEEF TEA WITH ACID.

One and one-half pounds of beef from the round, cut
in small pieces; same quantity ice broken small. Let it
stand in a deep vessel twelve hours; strain thoroughly and
forcibly through a coarse towel. Boil quickly ten minutes
in a porcelain vessel. Let cool. Add one-half teaspoonful of acid, or acid phosphate, to a pint. Serve hot or cold.

OATMEAL GRUEL.

One-half a cup of coarse oatmeal, three cups boiling
water, one teaspoonful of salt, and cream. Add oatmeal
and salt to boiling water, and cook three hours in a double
boiler. Force through a strainer, dilute with cream, reheat and strain a second time. Serve with salt or sugar.

CREAMED EGGS.

⅛ glassful of chicken stock.   4 eggs.
⅛ glassful of cream.   ½ teaspoonful of salt.
            pepper to taste.

Heat together the cream and the stock in a double
boiler. Beat the eggs without separating, and stir into
it slowly. Stir until thick, season and serve. This is the
most nourishing preparation of eggs for an invalid.

CREAMED CALF BRAINS.

Parboil the brains. Blanch them and cut into small pieces. Put into a double boiler one tablespoonful of butter and a scant one of flour. Add half a pint of cream. Put in slowly the beaten yolk of one egg, stirring constantly. Season with salt and pepper, add the brains, cook three minutes, and serve on toast.

CREAMED CHICKEN.

One tablespoonful of butter and one of flour, and add to that half a pint of cream, a little salt, pepper, and celery salt and the meat from half a chicken which has been put through the meat grinder.

MUTTON BROTH.

Lean loin of mutton, one and one-half pounds, including bone. Three pints of water. Boil gently until tender, throwing in a little salt and onion, according to taste. Pour out broth into basin; when cold, skim off the fat. Warm up when wanted.

CHICKEN BROTH.

Chop up a small chicken, or half of a large fowl. Boil it, bones and all, with a blade of mace, a sprig of parsley, a tablespoonful of rice, and a crust of bread in one quart of water, for an hour, skimming it from time to time. Strain through a colander.

EGG LEMONADE.

Beat one egg with one tablespoonful of sugar until very light; stir in three tablespoonfuls cold water and the juice of a small lemon. Fill the glass with pounded ice and drink through a straw.

CREAM SOUP.

Take one quart of good stock, chicken or mutton; cut one onion into quarters, slice three potatoes very thin and put into the stock with a small piece of mace. Boil gently for an hour. Then strain out the onion and mace. The potatoes should by this time have dissolved in the stock. Add one pint of milk, a very little corn flour to make it about as thick as cream, and a little butter. This soup may be made with milk instead of stock, if a little cream is used with it.

WINE WHEY.

Put two pints of new milk in a saucepan and stir over a clear fire until nearly boiling. Then add one gill (two wineglassfuls) of sherry and simmer a quarter of an hour, skimming off the curd as it rises. Add one tablespoonful more of sherry and skim again for a few minutes. Strain through coarse muslin. May use two tablespoonfuls of lemon juice instead of wine if desired.

JUNKET.

Take one-half pint of fresh milk, heated lukewarm. Add one teaspoonful essence of pepsin and stir just enough to mix. Pour into custard cups and let it stand until firmly curded. Serve plain or with sugar and grated nutmeg. May add sherry.

RUM PUNCH.

White sugar two teaspoonfuls, one egg beaten up. Add a large wineglassful warm milk, two to four teaspoonfuls Jamaica rum, and a little nutmeg.

MILK AND EGGS.

Beat milk with salt to taste.   Beat white of egg until stiff.   Add egg to milk and stir.

CHAMPAGNE WHEY.

Boil one-half pint of milk.   Strain through cheesecloth and add one wineglass of champagne.

DAINTY MENUS

FOR CONVALESCENT PATIENTS

Select the daintiest of tray covers and china, and make
the tray look as attractive as possible in every way.

No. 1.

Bouillon.
Creamed Chicken on Toast,
garnished with parsley.
Small Mold Bavarian Cream
with whipped Cream.

No. 2.

Cream of Celery Soup.
Supreme of Chicken with White Sauce, garnished with
parsley.
Beaten Biscuit.
One Fresh Tomato, garnished with chopped celery or
Nasturtium leaves.
Mold of Wine Jelly.

No. 3.

Broiled Breast of chicken with drawn butter.
Creamed Sweetbreads on Toast with peas.
Bread and Butter Sandwiches.
A Cup of delicate chocolate.
A Little Whipped Cream, frozen.

No. 4.

An Orange cut in half, after being on ice several hours.
Broiled Sweetbread, garnished.
Quail on Toast.   Hot rolls.
Celery Salad, garnished with celery tops.
Bread Sticks.
Pineapple Ice.

No. 5.

Oyster Soup.
Broiled Beef Tenderloin, mushroom sauce.
Parisienne Potatoes.
Light Rolls.
Charlotte Russe.

No. 6.

Sweetbread Croquettes with Creamed peas.
Bread and Butter Sandwiches.
Celery Salad.
Chocolate with whipped cream.
Plain Ice Cream.

No. 7.

Shredded wheat biscuit toasted and served with
hot milk or cream.
(Serve in dainty pitcher).
Crisp Breakfast Bacon in parsley.
Hot Rolls.
Poached Egg on toast.
Breakfast cocoa.

No. 8.

Fresh Pineapple plugged, sugared; covered in crushed
ice, and garnish with mint leaves.
Broiled Breast of Chicken with drawn butter.
Beaten Biscuit.
Fresh Tomato (throughly chilled) garnished with
water cress, serve with dressing.
Strawberry sponge.

CHAPTER ON MENUS

SIMPLE LUNCHEON.

No. 1.

Sliced Pineapple with crushed ice and sherry.
Bouillon.
Oyster Patties.
Stuffed Lamb Chops with peas.
Egg Salad.
Brick cream and cakes.
Coffee.

No. 2.

Puree of Asparagus with whipped cream garnish.
Oysters en Coquille.
Chicken Croquettes with Creamed peas.
Hot Rolls.
Celery Salad. Wafers.
Bavarian Cream. Macaroons.
Coffee.

No. 3.

Tomato Puree.
Mushrooms a l'Algonquin on Toast.
Broiled Fillets. Potatoes en Surprise.
Hot Rolls.
Hollandaise Punch.
Pepper Timbals.
Chicken Salad, Cheese Straws.
Individual Orange Ice with Cakes.
Coffee.

No. 4.

Grape Fruit.
Bouillon.
Fish Croquettes with white sauce. Potatoes.
Broiled Quail on Toast with asparagus.
Hot Rolls.
Hollandaise Punch.
Little Pigs in Blankets (Sweetbreads).
Waldorf Salad. Wafers.
Individual Ices and cakes.
Coffee.

No. 5.

Large Pink Grapes served in crushed ice with sherry wine.
Lobster Cutlets with bechamel sauce.
Graham bread sandwiches.
Broiled Grouse.   Potatoes en Surprise with oyster Sauce.
Hot Rolls.
Victoria Punch.
Croquettes of French Peas with Sauce.
Salad a la Jardin.   Wafers.
Individual Brick.   Cake.
Coffee.

No. 6.

Oyster Bisque.
Fish Croquettes with Potatoes.
Rolled Bread and Butter.
Broiled Quail.   Saratoga Chips.
Asparagus.   Beaten biscuit.
Punch.
Supreme of Chicken with bechamel sauce.
Green Grape Salad.   Cheese Wafers.
Ice Cream with Brandied Fruit. Cakes.
Coffee.

INFORMAL DINNER

No. 1.

Salted Almonds. Olives.
Chicken Gumbo.
Fish Pudding. Parisienne Potatoes.
Graham Bread and Butter.
Roast Turkey, Cranberry Sauce. Croquettes of Peas. Hot Rolls.
Asparagus and Stuffed Sweet Potatoes.
Celery Salad. Cheese Sticks.
Charlotte Russe or Ices.
Coffee.

No. 2.

Salted Almonds, Pickles and Celery.
St. Germain Soup
Broiled Pompano. Potatoes au Gratin. Beaten Biscuit.
Grouse or Pheasant. Asparagus. Peas. Hot Rolls.
Nut and Celery Salad. Wafers.
Fig Pudding with fancy sauce.
Cakes.

No. 3.

Salted Pecans.   Stuffed Olives.
Consomme.   Croutons.
Baked Fish.   Duchess Potatoes.   Beaten Biscuit.
Roast Fillet of Beef.   Brussels Sprouts.   Stuffed Tomatoes.   Rolls.
Cucumber and Celery Salad.   Wafers.
Baked Caramel Custard.   Cake.
Coffee.

No. 4.

Salted Almonds.   Mints.
Frozen Fruit.
Cream of Celery Soup.   Bread Sticks.
Oyster Croquettes.   French Fried Potatoes.   Beaten Biscuit.
Broiled Quail or Broiled Chicken Breast with Mushrooms.
Asparagus Tips.   Stuffed Sweet Potatoes.   Rolls.
Green Grape and Nut Salad.   Wafers.
Sultana Roll and Claret Sauce.   Cake.
Coffee.

No. 5.

Salted Pecans.   Mints.
Grape Fruit.
Cream of Pea Soup.   Buttered Toast.
Salpicon of Lobster in Patty Shells.
Lamb Chops a la Maintenon.   Parisienne Potatoes.   Hot Rolls.
Sweet Bread, Cucumber and Celery Salad.   Cheese Sticks.
Montrose Pudding with sauce.   Cakes.
Coffee.

No. 6.

Salted Almonds.   Mints.
Pineapple Sherbert, Creme de menthe Cherries.
Cream of Asparagus Soup.   Crackers.
Soft Shell Crabs.   Beaten Biscuit.   Cucumbers.
Stuffed Peppers.   Rolls.   Peas.
Pineapple and Nut Salad.   Cheese Wafers.
Nesselbrode Pudding.   Cakes.
Coffee.

DINNER

No. 1.

Salted Almonds.   Maron Glace.
Blue Points on Half Shell.
Consomme.
Lobster Timbals with lobster sauce.
Brown Bread and Butter Sandwiches.
Fillet of Beef.   Parisienne Potatoes.   Asparagus.   Hot Rolls.
Victoria Punch.
Stuffed Quail.   Croquettes of Peas with white sauce.
Beaten Biscuit.
Stuffed Mushrooms.
Celery Salad.   Wafers.
Fancy Ices and Cakes.
Coffee.

No. 2.

Blue Points on Half Shell.
Consomme.
Stuffed Lobster.   Bread and Butter Sandwiches.
Fillet of Beef.   Creamed Cauliflower.   Potatoes.   Hot Rolls.
Roman Punch.
Broiled Grouse with Asparagus.
Beaten Biscuit.
Sweetbread Croquettes with peas.
Green Grape Salad.   Cheese Wafers.
Fancy Ices and Cakes.
Coffee.

No. 3.

Oyster Cocktail.
Cream of Celery Soup with whipped cream garnish.
Lobster a la Newburg.   Graham Bread Sandwiches.
Venison Steaks.   Asparagus.   Hot Rolls.
Roman Punch.
Sweetbread a la Victoria, allemande sauce.   Peas.
Salad a la Jardin, in turnips.   Wafers.
Sultana Roll Ice with claret sauce.   Cakes.
Coffee.

No. 4.

Caviare on Toast.
Consomme.
Lobster Timbals.   Bread and Butter Sandwiches.
Fillet of Beef.   Stuffed Sweet Potatoes.   Asparagus.   Hot Rolls.
Fruit Punch.
Pheasant.   Potatoes en Surprise with sauce.   Beaten Biscuit.
Stuffed Mushrooms.
Waldorf Salad.   Cheese Sticks.
Fancy Ices and Cake.
Coffee.

No. 5.

Salted Nuts. Mints.
Anchovy Eggs.
Oyster Bisque. Crackers.
Baked Fish. Potatoes. Cucumbers. Bread.
Stuffed Chicken Leg. Peas. Hot Rolls.
Victoria Punch.
Individual Fillet with Mushrooms.
Cauliflower au Gratin. Rolls.
Green Pepper and Grape Fruit Salad. Cheese Ramequins.
Brandy Peaches with Vanilla Cream. Cakes.
Coffee.

No. 6.

Fresh Strawberries with caps,
served on shaved ice, powdered sugar (served in paper cups).
Bouillon. Croutons.
Soft Shell Crabs or Lobster Cutlets. Cucumbers in cucumber
cups. Beaten Biscuit.
Chicken Livers en Brochette, sauce. Bread and Butter Sandwiches.
Hollandaise Punch.
Broiled Chicken. French Pea Croquettes.
Broiled Tomatoes. Hot Rolls.
Water Cress and Orange Salad. Cheese Sticks.
Individual Ices. Cakes.
Coffee.